The Trouble with HR

An Insider's Guide to Finding and Keeping the Best Talent

JOHNNY C. TAYLOR, JR. AND GARY M. STERN

HARPERCOLLINS
LEADERSHIP

AN IMPRINT OF HARPERCOLLINS

The Trouble with HR

Published by HarperCollins Leadership,
an imprint of HarperCollins Focus LLC.

Any internet addresses, phone numbers, or company or product information printed in this book are offered as a resource and are not intended in any way to be or to imply an endorsement by HarperCollins Leadership, nor does HarperCollins Leadership vouch for the existence, content, or services of these sites, phone numbers, companies, or products beyond the life of this book.

Bulk discounts available. For details visit:
www.harpercollinsleadership.com/bulkquotes
Email: customercare@harpercollins.com

ISBN 978-1-4002-3250-5 (TP)

CONTENTS

CONTENTS

iii

♦ ♦ ♦

THE CONTEXT OF TALENT

By

Wayne Brockbank, Clinical Professor, Ross School of Business at the University of Michigan; Partner, The RBL Group

It is fortuitous that a book on talent management appears in the midst of the most serious economic difficulty in two generations. However, this book goes beyond specific issues related to talent and addresses issues relative to the strategies and activities of effective HR departments and to the attributes and behaviors of effective HR leaders. A major contribution of this work is successful integration of talent management, HR strategy, and fundamental leadership. With substantive insights, relevant examples, and practical tools, Taylor and Stern weave their work through the realities of business in general and, in a timely manner, through the economic turbulence of our day.

The basic premise of their work is that talent always matters. In good times, talent is the driver of growth and prosperity. In difficult times, talent is the key mechanism through which companies earn their way back to top-line and bottom-line success. But in difficult times our skill at talent management becomes more keenly tested. As has been stated by many business writers, "Positive cash flow covers a multitude of operational sins." When things are difficult, as they surely are today, the true character, intelligence, and relevance of our institutions, practices, and leadership capabilities are revealed. Today's context provides the opportunity and the mandate to critically examine all that HR professionals and leaders do. As has been suggested by several business thinkers, "A crisis is a terrible thing to waste." There was never a more important time to critically examine how we can better identify, obtain, retain, and utilize talent, how we can develop more powerful, relevant, and focused HR strategies, and how we need to function as leaders not just for HR but for the business as a whole. Such is the mandate of our times.

We are in the midst of a financial crisis. What role did HR practices play? HR practices did not account for the long run, for the integrated, holistic picture, for the impact on others, and for the unanticipated consequences. The unregulated and unbridled greed of individuals was jettisoned by ill-conceived and -executed HR practices.

This may be placing unfair expectations and responsibility on HR. It might be asked, "Is it fair to expect HR professionals to know and understand the entire business context in which they operate—especially when that context includes the complicated world of macro financial structures and practices on a global scale?" The response is, "Of course! What is the alternative?"

What are the implications of this current state of affairs for talent management?

One irony of business is that the worse things get, the greater the importance for companies to focus on the talent agenda. But under difficult and challenging conditions, the logic of talent management must be transformed to track the contextual changes that determine the eventual relevance of talent management and any other HR practice. In a recent issue of *BusinessWeek* (January 19, 2009), a list of the best and worst managers for 2008 are suggested. One of the most frequent accomplishments of the best managers was their focus on the core: identifying the core of their businesses, doing the core with excellence, and reducing nonessential tasks. As you will find, this is one of the core messages of *The Trouble with HR*. The current crisis provides a substantial and credible opportunity to do what companies should have been doing all along: identifying the core activities that create the greatest value for customers and shareholders, ensuring that the best people are doing the most valuable work with excellence, and reducing or eliminating the rest. Thus, one might argue that there has never been a war for talent; rather, there has always been a war for the best talent in the most valuable positions. In sum, now is the time to reconfigure your talent pool based on customer-focused value creation. The concepts and tools for so doing are in this book.

Whereas talent focuses on ensuring the recruitment, retention, and utilization of individuals, the overall HR strategy focuses on both individual talent as well as on organizational capability. Creating outstanding organizational capability enables the company as a whole to be more valuable than the sum of its parts. The framing of this agenda may be provided by the following question:

"Is it possible to have five world-class basketball players and not have a world-class basketball team?" The answer is a resounding, "Obviously!" A focus on organizational capabilities enables that agenda to occur. Organizational capability includes constructs such as speed, innovation, efficiency, quality, and accountability. Organizations that unify themselves around these capabilities and execute with excellence are much more likely to win. However, in today's environment another organizational capability must also receive extraordinary attention: the creation and maintenance of a powerful and robust corporate culture.

In today's environment the rules of the business game are shifting. HR must focus on creating and sustaining cultures that are flexible, resilient, mutually supportive, integrated, and creative. Institutional survival will depend on these cultural characteristics.

A most compelling section of this book is found in the chapter on leadership. It builds on the premise that HR professionals cannot credibly and expertly be responsible for developing business leaders if they themselves are not credible and expert business leaders. This is an essential contribution of Taylor and Stern. In the traditional leadership development model, HR professionals providing training to leaders on identifying a vision and strategy, making key decisions, ensuring a structure that is consistent with the strategy, aligning people, processes, and practices with the strategy, measuring results, and making appropriate adjustments. This model works exceptionally well as long as the vision and strategy are clear and explicit. The problem is that (as mentioned above) no one knows exactly how to manage our way out of the current turmoil. Therefore, the traditional leadership models are less useful. What is the alternative? Taylor and Stern boldly offer that the alternative is *Courage*.

- *Courage to be resilient*. In the midst of the battle, people need leaders who are emotional and physically resilient. They need leaders who do not allow turbulence on the outside of themselves to create turbulence within themselves. They need leaders who are role models of personal stability in the face of crisis.

- *Courage to be confident*. Today's leaders may not know the answers but they must have confidence in themselves and in their people so that they, together, can work their way through the crisis. They reflect their confidence in public statements as well as in private settings. Paradoxically, a powerful expression of confidence is in their personal humility. Confident humility allows a leader to acknowledge that she or he does not have all the answers but also allows the leader to express confidence that the answers will come forth. They acknowledge that the answers may come from themselves, from their teams, or from the organization as a whole. When the answers do come forth, they give extensive credit to others.

- *Courage to be flexible*. Facing the unknown requires the courage to be flexible, the courage to change. It requires the intellectual and emotional stamina to shift gears and to be willing to shift gears. It requires the capacity to wisely experiment at a personal level as well as at an institutional level. But, again paradoxically, today's leaders must convey a sense of personal and institutional stability around core values while managing with flexibility into the future.

☞ *Courage to put oneself at risk.* By definition if there is no downsize personal risk, there is no courage. People need leaders with this kind of courage. There is evidence in some companies that this courage is evident. I visited yesterday with a close friend who is the president of a point of purchase advertising company. He has around 175 employees. He asked everyone to take a 10 percent pay cut; the members of his leadership team took a 20 percent pay cut; he took a 50 percent pay cut. He knows that his people are at risk and he has placed himself at risk. This seems to be the kind of courage that is needed, as opposed to the $18 billion in bonuses that Wall Street has announced for its executives while thousands of their colleagues are being laid off.

☞ *Courage to be optimistic and realistic.* Paradox inserts itself again. Today's leaders must be role models of optimism. But they must also publicly and privately acknowledge that they face unprecedented difficulties. As Jim Morgan, the chairman of Applied Materials, has stated, "Good news is news; no news is bad news; bad news is good news." If this was a true business axiom when originally stated several years ago, it is certainly more relevant today. Successful leaders must find good news in identifying problems and seeking for solutions with realism and optimism.

Why is this kind of courage needed in leaders today? The primary reason is that courage is not only needed by leaders but this kind of courage is needed by everyone. In today's world everyone must be optimistic but realistic, must be willing to put themselves at risk, must be flexible at the margin and stable at the core, must concurrently be confident and humble, and must be physically and emotionally resilient. These are difficult capabilities to acquire. But effective leaders embody them and serve as visible and credible role models of these critical attributes.

This book, *The Trouble with HR*, provides insights, examples, and practical tools to help HR professionals and line leaders to address issues of talent management, HR strategy, and leadership. I wish you the best in your reading of this important book.

CHAPTER ONE

♦ ♦ ♦

GUIDE TO CHOOSING THE RIGHT PEOPLE: THE TEN MAJOR HIRING MISTAKES AND WHAT TO DO ABOUT THEM

Anticipating your client's changing needs. Adapting to a global environment. Thinking outside the box. You could make a case these skills are necessary to keep your company one step ahead of competitors. But there is one major skill that most experts overlook that may be the ultimate decider of how your business or organization does in the coming years: hiring the right people. Arguably, if you don't hire the right people—and retain them— you won't be able to devise new products, meet customer needs, and sustain the business.

Most CEOs and business leaders spend ample time on their marketing plans and financial projections. Most often they leave hiring up to the business managers who devote the same energy and research to recruiting the right staff as they do ordering paper clips. Recruiting new staff is often considered an afterthought, something to attend to after the "primary" tasks get done. Many hiring executives view human resources and the HR function as an impediment, a department responsible for filing paperwork away in steel cabinets, forcing performance appraisals on them, and adding little value. Rather than serving as a support staff and adding value for recruiting and hiring, HR is often ignored. *The Trouble with HR: An Insider's Guide to Finding and Keeping the Best Talent* makes the case that organizations must take a new approach to managing their human resources because, in an increasingly competitive and global economy, the key to future success and growth is simple: Hire the right people and retain them.

Too many organizations hire for the minute and never think about long-term retention. For some reason, for-profit and not-for-profit entities, as well as government agencies, continue to believe that it makes sense to be reactive as opposed to proactive when it comes to managing what they all claim to be "our most important asset." Business, nonprofit, and government leaders alike must understand why hiring the right people, and being able to retain them, is so critical to the bottom-line performance of their organizations. Consider the following:

1. The U.S. Bureau of Labor Statistics reports that in 2012, a mere three years away, there will be 165 million jobs but only 162 million people to fill them. Holding on to your talented staff will become increasingly significant as baby boomers retire and the difficulty replacing them intensifies.

2. The article "Making Talent a Strategy Priority," in the January 2008 issue of *The McKinsey Quarterly*, written by Matthew Guthfride, Asmus B. Komm, and Emily Lawson, attests to the role that hiring the right people and retaining them plays in a company's future. "Vying for

top talent in an intensively competitive global marketplace" will become a major strategic initiative for most companies, according to the authors. Organizations will have to begin to see and use human capital "in a focused, deliberate, and proactive way to optimize the workforce." The article makes clear that most companies are currently ill equipped to take advantage of their human capital and that companies that do better at retaining employees will have an easier time competing for global talent than the organizations that ignore turnover: "Measure turnover, understand its causes, and design programs to control it to reduce vacancy costs—both financial and productivity—to avoid its devastating affect on business."

3. In an October 2005 *Harvard Business Review* article, "Growing Talent as If Your Business Depended on It," the authors, Jeffrey M. Cohn, Rakesh Khurana, and Laura Reeves, cite a survey of twenty CEOs who said that having the right talent in the right roles was paramount to their companies' success and that a talent management program was important for developing effective leaders. Sadly, however, nearly half of those very CEOs admitted that they had no succession plans or retention strategies for vice presidents and above—the most critical group of employees on their bench.

The Retention Imperative

Retention is not something organizations can *choose* to do if they want to be viable, successful entities in the future. The organizations that can hold onto their staff, develop them into leaders, move them up the organization, create a steady flow of talent, and not spend the bulk of their time on replacing talent will WIN. And since winning is the name of the game, there must be a *retention imperative*. And we need leaders to create an environment where staff is recognized, development becomes a natural part of business, and staff wants to stay.

At the companies where turnover predominates and making people a priority is given only lip service, productivity falters. Not only that, but line managers spend more of their time on recruitment and hiring and less time devoted to their business and revenue growth.

Developing a Whole New Outlook on Hiring and Retaining

Though two of us, Johnny C. Taylor, Jr and Gary M. Stern, collaborated on this book, we're going to draw on the experiences of Taylor, who has been a general counsel, an HR director, and CEO of RushmoreDrive.com, a new Internet site and community. Hence we're going to write it in first person from Taylor's viewpoint, though the two of us wrote the book.

So I'm often asked what's more important—hiring or retention? And like any good lawyer, I say both. The fact of the matter is that they are equally important. It is classic tomfoolery to focus on retaining employees who should have never made it into your organization in the first place. If you hire the wrong people and then hold onto them, your organization will fail. And if you hire the right people and can't hold onto them, your organization will suffer just as much. Hence, a strong hiring strategy is a prerequisite to a successful employee retention strategy.

Hiring the best people requires a whole new hiring approach. Until recently, the common practice, whether in Fortune 500 multinationals, small and midsize businesses, not-for-profits, or government agencies, was for most hiring to be done on a stopgap, emergency, "filling the vacancy" basis. Someone left for a better job, and the company ratcheted up efforts to hire a replacement. In a knowledge economy, when millions of baby boomers are retiring each year, the quick-fix hiring effort no longer works.

Instead, as this book suggests, there is a better way, an entirely different and very deliberate approach to recruiting and retaining people over the life cycle of an employee's stay at the organization. The approach keeps everyone involved. That way, when you need someone to step in to fill a vacancy, you already know the strengths of your internal employees and who can advance into managerial or leadership positions.

In a sense, organizations have to operate more like sports teams. Every football team knows that it has a forty-man squad, a "taxi" squad with five additional players, and is constantly searching for qualified talent to fill positions in case of injuries. Football teams recognize that the best talent wins games and those players are constantly in and out of games due to injuries, trades, or deteriorating skills. Too many businesses, on the other hand, have adopted the "ostrich" approach—keeping their head in the sand and ignoring hiring decisions until the emergency happens.

When most people think of hiring and retaining staff, they think first of Fortune 500 and other major corporations. But nearly everything that we focus on in this book—creating a long-term hiring strategy, identifying talent, interviewing based on a detailed job description, fitting the job with the candidate, hiring for the future—is as true for the military, nonprofit organizations, and small businesses as for large public corporations. Because most nonprofits and small businesses cannot offer stock options and have some restrictions on bonuses compared to public companies, these organizations must focus on making the job appealing, providing more autonomy, giving staff more challenges, and compensating for the lack of financial incentives.

I've been a senior HR executive of a Fortune 500 company, general counsel for major corporations, and I am now a CEO of an Internet start-up, RushmoreDrive.com, a new IAC/InterActive Corp. subsidiary, targeted toward African Americans. Over the years, in addition to my "day job," I've also served as chairman of the Society for Human Resource Management (SHRM), an organization of more than 250,000 professionals and the largest HR organization in the world. In short, I've hired and fired executives, advised organizational leaders on who to hire, identified and recruited people, and then arranged strategies to retain them. I've done hiring and recruited talent from a 360-degree perspective, and one key thing I have learned is that if you don't figure out a strategy to get your hiring right, you won't get your work done. Hiring the right people enables you to stay one step ahead of your competitors. If you don't recruit the right people, you are spending too much time and too many dollars replacing them, and your competitors will eat your lunch.

Nor am I only referring to hiring senior executives. If you don't hire the right customer service or call center staff, or even an executive assistant for a senior vice president, for example, you can lose customers and money. Your reputation can suffer when your company, via customer complaints and feedback on the Internet and blogs, becomes known as a firm that doesn't care about customer service. Hiring right at every level boosts your company's bottom line, productivity, and performance, no matter its size.

Most leaders and entrepreneurs know that many businesses fail because they are undercapitalized. But they are usually referring to financial capital. What they overlook is many businesses fail because they lack sufficient *human* capital. Had the entrepreneur been more knowledgeable about how to invest capital, the business might have stayed afloat. Often, the lack of human capital— hiring the wrong manager, choosing the wrong staff, not retaining staff, failing to develop a consistent customer service approach— derails entrepreneurial efforts faster than financial woes. Just focusing on inadequate financial capital misses the big picture.

Perhaps Michael D. Brown, the former director of the Federal Emergency Management Agency (FEMA), best exemplifies how hiring the wrong leader can undermine an organization. Brown started as director of FEMA in January 2003 and resigned in September 2005. Before joining FEMA, he was the commissioner of the International Arabian Horse Association from 1989–2001, a position that did not provide him with the requisite background, experience, or skills to handle a major crisis such as Hurricane Katrina. In fact, he had no emergency management experience before joining FEMA. Because Brown was overwhelmed and ill equipped to do the job he'd been chosen to do, many people lost their lives.

What we had at FEMA was a failure to hire someone based on skill and competence. From the marbled halls of Congress to the cherry-paneled walls in corporate offices on Wall Street, fielding the wrong team of players results in failure

What price do companies pay for their hiring mistakes? The SHL Group, a London-based company that produces psychometric assessment products, and The Future Foundation conducted a study of 700 global managers to quantify the actual cost of turnover and inadequate hiring. The study revealed that companies wasted $105 billion a year worldwide on replacing staff, an amount equivalent to one percent of the U.S. gross domestic product.

In the SHL study, Lawrence Karsh, president of SHL Americas, noted that while many CEOs insist people are their most importance resource, the fact of the matter is that they don't act on that idea very often. On one hand, CEOs proclaim that people are their most important asset, while on the other hand, Karsh said, they refused to sufficiently invest in their talent acquisition departments or the training and professional development of their management personnel.

Coleman Peterson, the former head of HR at Wal-Mart, has said in speeches that the formula for success revolves around three things: "getting good people, keeping people, and growing good people." And Jim Collins, in his book *Good to Great*, wrote, "People are not your most important asset; the right people are."

The entire world has changed. What worked in the past in recruiting staff is likely to be ineffective today. Globalization, for example, has turned hiring specialized staff into an international competition; knowledge workers such as IT professionals, software engineers, scientists, and financial service experts are in demand in London, Geneva, New York, and Beijing. In the recent past, the Fortune 100 could go to any of the nation's most elite colleges and universities and have their pick of the litter. Now, just a few years later, they not only have to fight the other ninety-nine companies that make up the Fortune 100 for talent, but they have to fight to keep that talent from the FTSE 100 companies in the United Kingdom and Japan's Nikkei 100.

Hiring the Right People Occurs at Every Level of the Organization

When organizations have to hire a new senior leader, they often hire a leading executive recruiting search firm and spend hundreds of thousands of dollars in the pursuit of the right person. Boards understand this money is well spent. However, these very organizations often overlook the importance of hiring the right people at every level, not just at the top.

For example, when I was senior vice president of HR at IAC/InterActive Corp., I had the not-so-easy task of hiring an executive assistant for CEO Barry Diller. A very demanding CEO (are there any other kind?), Diller was a dynamic and visionary boss. Identifying the right executive assistant for him was difficult. Though many people overlook administrative assistants, Diller's assistant played a key role in the organization.

When I oversaw the job search, I zeroed in on a candidate with three attributes: the right skills, personality, and attitude. The applicant had to meet these three criteria or I'd keep looking—and it didn't matter how long it took because we needed to find the right person. (Notice where I'm going here?) Finding someone with the right skills was the easiest of the three requirements because the executive assistant needed to have high-level computer skills and the ability to interpret material, type quickly, and multitask. The more difficult part was finding someone who had energy and piz-zazz that could match Diller's intensity level. Since Diller was de-manding and blunt at times, I needed someone with a thick skin who wouldn't wilt at an occasional slight.

Furthermore, the executive assistant didn't just have to get along well with Diller. This individual also had to deal effectively with other leaders in media. If Robert Iger, CEO of Walt Disney Company, or Summer Redstone, CEO of Viacom, called, the ex-ecutive assistant would have to be equipped to handle these high-powered leaders. If you combined all of the ingredients required for this job, merging highly developed computer and interpersonal skills, you'd realize it wasn't an easy person to find. My point is simple: Even though you may not spend thousands of dollars on an executive recruiter to find an administrative assistant, recruiting for these positions still takes time and care.

Avoiding a Short-Term Focus

Where do most executives go wrong in their hiring? Most hiring managers focus only on hiring, and although it may sound ironic, that's one of the biggest and most common mistakes. What they need to focus on is long-term retention. Just hiring someone to fill a position that's going to turn over in six months to a year is a waste of time and energy. If you are only focused on hiring, you are going to make a mistake. I like to refer to what business managers should be concentrating on as the *life cycle* of an employee's stay at the company or organization. Focus on hiring the right person and identifying a new employee who will most likely stay in the position for several years until the time comes to move up or out.

I recommend a "holistic" hiring approach. Write a detailed job description and focus on the person's attributes and cultural fit—not just skills. Let's say the applicant for a job in finance is a phenomenally skilled accountant, but is passive, lethargic, and moves slowly. If the hiring manager is an intense, hard-driving, type A individual, we may not have a good fit. Moreover, if the culture at the organization demands finding new solutions and the applicant is a plodding individual who prefers taking orders to showing initiative, it won't be a good fit, even if the person has an MBA from an Ivy League school.

Developing a *"people competency"* in your organization is critical to your success. From a "business" perspective, we understand the concept that different organizations are known for having different competencies. Some are known for having branding and marketing competency (Coca-Cola); customer service competency (Nordstrom and Southwest Airlines); innovation and technological competency (Google); discipline and execution competency (U.S. military branches); and talent competency (the Ford Foundation). But few organizations have achieved a people competency—a fact that I find particularly startling given that nearly every CEO, owner, director, or officer says people are their most important asset.

If Coca-Cola is going to achieve its business goals, appeal to its customers, expand its audience, and move beyond its dependence on one major product, it will need competent marketing people. When companies succeed, often the very people who made it happen are overlooked. If Coca-Cola or PepsiCo develops a new designer water, for example, it wasn't just the company's strategy that got the job done. At the risk of sounding glib, it's the people stupid. One of the most important things these companies can do is to put the right people in the right jobs. Product designers, marketers, advertisers, and sales combined to develop a product, decided how to sell it, and convinced customers to buy it. The staff deserves the credit, as do the people that hired this staff, just as scouts in baseball are recognized for noticing the talent of a rookie prospect. Omar Minaya, currently the general manager of the New York Mets, was given credit for scouting and discovering Sammy Sosa on a dirt field in the Dominican Republic. Sosa went on to hit over 500 home runs playing in the major leagues.

Hire the right people. Choose people that fit into your dynamic culture. Make sure people can work together to bring out the best in each other. These are the business imperatives that determine our success, and it is why Coca-Cola would be well served by having a people competency.

But choosing the right people is only the starting point. After an employer selects the right people, it must inspire them to become part of the organization's vision. Every single employee, from the VP of technology to the marketing manager to administrative assistants, plays a role in creating the company and moving it toward achievement of its business goals.

Why did Southwest Airlines vanquish American, United, Delta, and Continental? Herb Kelleher, Southwest's original CEO, had a vision that creating a fun corporate culture where people wanted to go to work would boost corporate revenue. His mantra: If employees aren't happy, they can't make customers happy. Disgruntled employees can never meet customer needs. Why did Starwood Hotels and its W subsidiary develop a boutique hotel that has been emulated by the industry? For a company to demonstrate people competency, it must exhibit five characteristics:

1. Establish a consistent talent acquisition process that reflects the organization's identity.

2. Reward their people financially and nonfinancially.

3. Treat their people right and make them feel respected and valued.

4. Train their people.

5. Develop their best into leaders.

In his book *Winning*, Jack Welch says the most important person in your organization is not your CFO who handles the finances, but your top HR executive who oversees hiring and training people. If you don't hire the right people for the long term, your finances and revenues won't be in order, no matter who your CFO is. That's because sales will plummet and, without the right people, the company will lose its competitive edge.

Hiring Is Only the Beginning

Of course, hiring the right person is only the first step. What's key (and I'll focus more on these issues in chapter 3 on retention) is keeping people. And that entails managing people so they grow and develop, compensating them with the right pay and benefits, and recognizing them for their hard work. Several HR studies have shown that pay raises boost employee morale, but usually only for a limited time. Recognizing staff members for their efforts and letting them know how their accomplishments fit into the organization's overall goals sustain them for the long haul. I recommend focusing on training your weaker employees to improve their skills and developing your A-list performers into leaders. Training involves mastering the skills on the job, and development entails learning new skills on jobs you will hold in the future.

Recruiting in Smaller Companies and Not-for-Profits

Identifying the right employee is arguably more important in the organization of fifteen to twenty people than it is at the multinational corporation with 130,000 employees. If your small-to-medium-sized organization has two people in finance, and the CFO leaves for a better job, your number-two person better be strong, knowledgeable, and skilled or else your business will suffer. Since many smaller businesses don't have the financial resources to offer higher salaries, bonuses, and stock options like a multinational can, they must rely on more ingenious ways to woo employees and retain them.

One major advantage smaller businesses have is the lack of bureaucracy. Rather than having to go through four layers of approvals up to the senior vice president who must sign off on everything, smaller businesses often empower people to make decisions or confer with the owner to proceed. That appeals to people who are doers rather than people who prefer attending meetings, gaining approval, and operating as a subordinate, not a leader. That advantage of taking charge and gaining control over one's area can easily be stressed in interviewing.

Viewing Recruiting in a New Light

When companies compete for customers, they create elaborate advertising campaigns, PowerPoint demonstrations, and create a multidimensional marketing strategy to woo them. Compare and contrast the effort and resources they put into competing for the best talent to join the organization. There is no comparison. Unfortunate as it is, most organizations (I dare say nearly all) view recruiting and retaining staff as a necessary function—but nothing more. In a knowledge economy, when premium workers are often in the driver's seat and can choose among several suitors, organizations need a new approach—one that more closely mirrors how we pursue new customers.

For example, think about how auto dealers operate: They try to create a customer for life by selling a car to a twenty-eight-year-old, following up with vehicle services in order to sell the customer a new auto every four years. Having a customer for life can boost sales exponentially. Similarly, keeping an employee for the long term, rather than having a revolving door of employees, can spike productivity and reduce hiring costs.

Just as you try to convince a customer about the strengths, advantages, and competitive edge of your product or service, you must persuade your applicants that working for your company is the place to be. Treating them with respect, being on time, listening to them, asking them questions, and responding quickly to their questions are all ways to establish a relationship with them that can turn them into long-term employees.

When I interview job candidates, I assume from the beginning they are qualified. If these applicants weren't qualified, they wouldn't have made it past that initial vetting. My talent acqui-sition professional has already screened fifty resumes and narrowed down the choice to the top-three people. I'm not trying to estab-lish whether they possess the skills, I'm trying to ascertain if they are a good fit for the company.

For example, a start-up CEO/entrepreneur may be in a diffi-cult marketplace with tough competitors and face new challenges every day. If the owner interviews someone who says leaving work at 5 p.m. is a priority, the odds are strong that the owner is going to choose someone else who stays late and does what it takes to get the job done. Start-up cultures demand working hard and being flexible and being rewarded for that. So, it is critical that this CEO focus on finding someone who fits that company's culture.

Competing for talent against established brands is a challenge. Established brands can offer stock options, perquisites, and larger of-fices with snazzier furniture than smaller companies can. How then can I recruit people? We hire people who see themselves as "intrapre-neurs." Yes, they work for a Fortune 500 company, IAC, but when it comes to our start-up Internet business, they must treat every dollar as their own. Unlike at larger financial services companies, where five layers of bureaucracy are needed to authorize a new project or marketing plan, we need people who are industrious, take control, can be assertive, and act as entrepreneurs within our company.

Where Most People Go Wrong in Hiring

Why do so many companies often choose the wrong candidates who last a short time? People naively think that hiring is easy and intuitive. Consequently, they think hiring can be done in a cursory way. All they need to do is place an ad in *The Wall Street Journal* or post their job opening on an online job posting site, review a hundred resumes, cull them down to three leading candidates, interview them, and voila, the right candidate will appear. If only hiring were that easy or simplistic, everyone could do it. But the truth is, most people don't know how to hire effectively and, all too often, they base hiring decisions on very subjective and nebulous criteria (which I'll cover more in chapter 4, "Objectifying the Job Search"), leading to excessive and costly turnover.

If most managers were doing a presentation on their marketing or financial plans for the year, they'd organize their thoughts, plan it out, and conduct extensive research. But most hiring managers think choosing the right candidate can be done by soliciting a few resumes and relying on the chemistry between two people. The manager thinks, "The two of us get along; I like the candidate, and the candidate has the right resume. That's enough to go on." It's not.

Most hiring managers also misuse, belittle, or overlook the one resource that could help them identify the right talent: human resources. Long demeaned and often disregarded, HR can become your ally and a value-added resource in creating a well-thought-out strategy to identify the right staff members and retain them, two ingredients to long-lasting success. But rather than rely on HR, most executives dismiss it.

Why is HR so often ignored?

I knew a senior editor (I'll call him Phil), who worked at a major American publishing house. When I asked how he partnered with HR at his company when he needed to identify and recruit a new editor, he scoffed at my question. "Why would I confer with Andrea in HR on the sixth floor?" he said contemptuously. "What assistance could she offer?" Here's what Phil overlooks. He has paid no attention to turnover statistics and exit interviews. He isn't interested to know why people leave and why every year his publishing house has to hire eight new editors out of twenty, far above the industry norm. He has never investigated hiring trends or focused on what it takes to retain editors. Moreover, he doesn't study the competition or do market intelligence (more about that later). What he's missing is the contribution that a progressive, problem-solving HR professional can bring to a company.

To be fair, HR has had its failings and limitations. As the former chairman of the Society for Human Resource Management, I admit that many HR professionals could do a better job. But to dismiss them entirely and scoff at the role HR can play is to miss an opportunity to create a dynamic hiring strategy. I'll talk more about using HR as a resource in chapter 7.

To help hiring managers, senior executives, entrepreneurs, and directors of smaller companies and nonprofits, here are the ten major mistakes that I see in hiring and solutions for how to fix them.

Mistake 1: Management Thinks It's in Control

Management believes that it is calling the shots and it controls hiring. Ten to fifteen years ago, when baby boomers caused a surplus of workers, this attitude might have been the case—but no longer. Now the best and the brightest workers are in great demand. Try recruiting an engineer, financial analyst, registered nurse, or high-end auto mechanic, and see who's courting whom.

In the Internet age, company insiders can readily reveal private data about their company's culture, so candidates for jobs are spending as much time evaluating you as you are evaluating them. Generations X and Y and people in their twenties are armed with so much Internet knowledge that they come to the interview knowing the ins and outs and secrets of most companies.

Interviewers need to be prepared to explain the company's culture, where the new hires will fit into the company, and exactly what is expected of them. Interviewers must be more adept at role-playing, asking candidates how they would handle certain real-life situations. This type of exchange provides much better insight into the candidate than saying "Tell me about your background" or "Tell me why you're right for the job," which places the onus on the candidate. Those days are over. Hiring has become a reciprocal, two-way process.

Solution 1: Creating a Talent Acquisition Strategy

The best way to overcome the mistake of thinking you are in control when you're not is to create a talent acquisition strategy, whether between HR and the business or, if you're a smaller business, between a consultant and the entrepreneur. It starts with looking at hiring as a process, not just a one-time event to fill a position. When both experts—the HR expert who knows about hiring and the manager who has product and business knowledge—join forces, a stronger talent acquisition strategy can be developed. Working together, the duo can determine a realistic job description and exactly the qualities sought in the new position. If it is a marketing manager, for example, how much experience is required? What previous skills are desirable? What companies are you targeting?

I always create a list of three high-performing companies that are in the same industry as my company. I'd like to pursue their best employees. I also have in mind three companies in the industry that are falling behind, whose performers won't interest me because they are industry laggards.

Working with the business manager, we agree on a strategy of how we are going to identify candidates and the qualities that will best fit, and then map out a retention strategy to keep the person even before being hired.

Mistake 2: Making a Hiring Decision Based on a Resume and References

Many hiring managers find themselves impressed by a candidate's resume, past employer, and references. Each one of these is a trap that can derail the process of choosing the right candidate. Why? It's not the resume that should determine a hire, but a combination of the person's core skills, past experience, and ability to fit into the new company's culture. Most references obfuscate more than they reveal.

Solution 2: Using the Resume and References as a Starting Point Only

Resumes can be manipulated in a variety of ways. Most people have multiple resumes, noting how they specialize in accounting, finance, taxes, Sarbanes-Oxley, and consulting, for example. So-phisticated and trained HR professionals know how to read be-tween the lines, decipher the subtext, and ascertain what the real deal is about the skills of the candidates. Most business managers take resumes at face value; they are impressed by certain things and misled by others.

Most hiring managers review resumes in a cursory way. But if you are a seasoned HR professional, you learn to view those re-sumes skeptically. For example, on a research job search that I conducted, one candidate's resume described his being at a recent job from 2003–2004. On first glance, it would appear he spent two years on the job. But when I interviewed him, I asked him exactly when he started and left. It turns out that he started in November 2003 and left in January 2004. In reality, he lasted less than three months on the job. That information gave me the opportunity to ask what happened that caused him to resign. Most business man-agers might have accepted those two years as a longer term of em-ployment and missed following up on more revealing information.

Moreover, references are often written in code. In my experi-ence, few people ever write a straight reference. Most former man-agers want to play it safe. They don't want to say anything very revealing, so they stress the good and withhold the negative.

Mistake 3: Focusing on the Short-Term Only

Most business managers know only one thing: They need to fill a vacancy quickly. With everything on their plate, hiring is often put on the back burner. So they place an ad, review resumes quickly, interview three people, and make a decision. But there's one missing part of the equation: the position may get filled, and the candidate may possess the right skills, but will the person stay in the job? Will this job sustain the new hire, or will the person lose interest and jump ship? A look at the turnover statistics for new hires at most companies reveals that most managers hire short term and, as a result, get a temporary employee.

Solution 3: Choosing an Employee Who Will Stay and Grow

Dazzled by a resume and wanting to complete the hiring as quickly as possible to focus on their other tasks, many business managers leap at the first candidate whose background fits the job. Often these candidates are either overqualified or underqualified and don't last long, the job becoming just another steppingstone on someone's resume.

Bringing HR into the hiring process often means hiring an employee for the long term, which these days can mean five to seven years. HR can do the "intel," or market intelligence, on whether the candidate is likely to fit the job for several years, grow into the job, and expand skills as the business grows. Rather than looking for a temporary person to fill a void, HR concentrates on who can handle the job immediately, develop into the next job, and by moving up the corporation, help move it forward.

It needs to be a perfect match. As the former HR top executive of IAC/InterActive Corp., which owns Match.com, I know something about making matches, both in dating and hiring. If the HR person is clued in to the company's culture, understands it, and can project whether the candidate can fit into the culture, the HR specialist can make a likely projection of whether a new hire is going to last or fade away quickly. In this case, it's a business match, and that's one of the primary roles of the HR expert that helps to add value to hiring.

Mistake 4: Ignoring the Cultural Fit

I knew a CEO of a start-up financial services company who hired an accounting manager based on her resume. He was impressed by her skills and background and knew she could do the job. But when he interviewed her, he had doubts about how she would fit into the culture. She came across in the interview as having an edge. He sensed that her attitude could be a problem, but he was so impressed by her resume that he ignored the telltale signs and erased his own doubts.

On her first day on the job, she attended a meeting where she offended three of her colleagues. Angry, she stormed out of the meeting, leaving little room for compromise. Her first day was difficult, and it went downhill from there. She was replaced after six months. While a study by the American Management Association says replacement costs vary greatly depending on the job and salary, it estimates that most searches cost from 25 percent for lower-level positions to 200 percent of annual compensation for senior executives. Those costs include executive recruitment fees and customer service disruption.

Solution 4: Making a Cultural Match

Hiring someone with the right skills is a prerequisite. But it takes more than technical skills to thrive in most environments. Author

Daniel Goleman refers to these other skills as "emotional intelligence." Getting along with others, listening to what other people have to say, not getting bent out of shape by a slight reversal, and staying positive in the midst of setbacks are all signs of emotional intelligence.

During the interview, ask questions that will reveal how the applicant handles a crisis, whether the job seeker gets bent out of shape or takes things in stride. The applicant's answers might serve as indicators of emotional intelligence.

Culture will determine the kind of person you hire, and every corporate culture is different. Disney, for example, seeks people who can build relationships, since that's what the world of film and TV demands. At Hewlett-Packard, where 65 percent of sales derives from overseas operations, staff members who appreciate and value global diversity will likely thrive. If you know your culture, you must hire someone who can fit easily into it.

Don't be fooled by someone who has the right degree, impressive credentials, and all the right skills. If the person can't fit into your culture, all the skills that they possess won't be useful.

Mistake 5: Not Knowing Your Competition

Most hiring managers think that if they understand the job description and know their company, the hiring process will go smoothly. In most cases, they are mistaken. In addition to understanding your company's needs, you need to understand both the competition out there and the last company that the applicant has worked for in order to determine the best possible hire. Most business managers approach a job search in a myopic way, only focusing on their needs and not doing a competitive study.

Solution 5: Performing Market Intelligence

The odds are your best hiring will come from your competitors. And your best new recruits will come from your best competitors, not the also-rans. Keeping track of competitors requires market intelligence.

Hiring involves knowing the competition, as well as understanding your own culture. If you are hiring a position at a cutting-edge technology company, you must know the cultures at Google, Yahoo, or AOL to understand who the best candidates are.

If HR staffers are doing their job, they have their finger on the pulse, ear to the ground, and know what it's like to work at a competitor. Knowing both cultures is critical to hiring success.

If Universal is a culture that stresses working closely with clients in a collaborative way because the Hollywood culture is all relationship-driven and Sony focuses on self-initiators because the culture promotes creating new products, hiring someone from Universal may not make sense to Sony. While they may identify people who are skilled at forging relationships, they may not be good at working on their own and developing new products, and the new culture could clash with their skills.

Mistake 6: Asking Softball Questions

Most business managers who aren't trained in hiring ask questions such as, "Why are you right for this job?" and "What in your background prepares you for the job?" HR experts refer to these as softball questions because they are so open-ended they reveal little about the applicant and little about whether the person fits the job.

Solution 6: Role-Playing and Asking Revealing On-the-Job Questions

Instead of asking nebulous questions that reveal little, focus on specific questions that elicit how the applicant will handle real-life situations. If your star performer was acting disinterested in work, how would you handle it? If your boss asked you to do something that you considered unethical, what would you do? Let's role-play a performance appraisal. A member of your staff has underperformed and you want to help improve performance. What would you say or do?

What specific skills are you hiring for? Are you looking for a team player or a self-initiating salesperson who doesn't have to operate collaboratively? How do the answers from the role-play predict performance?

Mistake 7: Treating All Job Applicants as Your Mirror Image

Moreover, many hiring managers make the mistake of assuming that what keeps them at the company will keep their subordinate employees at the company, which is not the case. Driven, ambitious people need a clear path to the executive suite, but some other people will prefer job security and more time off.

When it comes to hiring, most managers follow the "do unto others as you would have them do unto you" rule. But that is dead wrong. Different people have different motivations.

Solution 7: Getting to the Root of an Employee's Motivation

Establishing the primary motivation for wanting to be hired is critical to determining whether the applicant is a good fit and likely to stay for several years or just turn into another turnover statistic. But often business managers overlook that vital question. That's like an engaged couple that never discussed whether they want to have children.

One of the key issues to elicit is why this applicant is attracted to this job. The answers will vary much more than people expect. For many people, each job is a steppingstone that moves them one step closer to becoming CFO, marketing director, or senior executive. How does this job enable the person to learn new skills? If the candidate wants a job that allows him to oversee a profit-generating division, but this job is in a support position, it might not be a good fit.

Some candidates seek a position that offers flexibility. As long as they can leave work early once a week to see their son or daughter play soccer, it could lead to a good fit. But if the job demands traveling ten days a month, that could cause conflict.

Other candidates prefer to work in a team environment while others are self-starters who prefer operating independently. Bringing all these issues out can help determine whether the applicant fits the job.

Mistake 8: Ignoring Key Motivators

Turnover produces innumerable problems for organizations. If someone is hired and leaves after a short stay, it can cost a company thousands of dollars in recruiter's fees and the cost of a job search. In addition, it can trigger morale issues because of the early exit. But many business managers fail to discover what will keep the person on the job for a longer term.

Solution 8: Focusing on the Long Term

Just hiring a person with the right skill set isn't enough—if you are thinking long term. What will make the applicant stay at the job is just as important as whether the applicant possesses the skills to do the job. If you hire them and they last a year, you have wasted considerable time and energy and then have to repeat the job search all over again.

What exactly will motivate the employee? Is it the training? Learning new tasks? The bonus? The ability to attend conferences? Taking a leadership position? Building their resume? Making contact with senior officials? Becoming a managing partner? Having a flexible work schedule?

First determine what will sustain the person in the organization. Then ascertain whether your company can deliver that. If not, find someone else.

Mistake 9: Managers Take Control of Hiring on Their Own

Many managers think they can perform the job search on their own and dismiss HR as an ally. Just like my editor friend Phil, many managers see HR as another layer of bureaucracy that gets in the way and adds minimal value. Why go through HR when you can use your contacts to identify the perfect candidate on your own? Why indeed!

What happens when the know-it-all manager places the ad and recruits the candidate on a solo trip into the hiring wilderness? Often the manager ends up hiring an employee who lasts less than a year and becomes a turnover statistic.

Solution 9: Collaborating with HR

What talented HR professionals bring to the recruiting search is *market intelligence*. HR professionals know the marketplace and understand which jobs will be difficult to fill. They know the competitive environment and where to find the best talent. For example, a savvy HR staff understands that Nike is a great brand with a talented merchandising staff, but Nike isn't known for its marketing department. If they are doing their job, HR professionals have contacts in talent acquisition to draw on that exceed one person's Rolodex.

Furthermore, the HR staff knows which companies and which specific departments have the best reputations, perform the most cutting-edge work, and attract the best employees. HR experts with market intelligence know which companies and which specific departments to avoid and which to recruit from. Identifying talent involves knowing the strengths and limitations of your competitors. A hiring manager in an academic setting looking to recruit a top ophthalmology professor would likely start the search process at Harvard University. If that hiring manager were collaborating with a highly trained HR professional who knew the market, he would have known that some of the best ophthalmology talent would be found at the University of Miami. Similarly, Google may have some of the best search engine scientists, but may be weak in marketing.

How Smaller Businesses Can Handle HR

If you're not GE or IBM and don't have the budget for a large HR department and, in fact, if your organization is very small and can't afford to hire a designated HR specialist, the tasks of recruiting and retaining still have to be done to keep your company chugging along and poised for future growth. Just as small businesses allocate a certain amount of funds for accounting and legal experience, setting aside some money for good HR advice is essential. A poor hiring decision in a small organization can do far more damage than most entrepreneurs and nonprofit directors can imagine. In many ways, the investment by a small business in an HR consultant to help identify good people, compensate them fairly, and pay them affordable benefits (which will help keep them around for a long time) is arguably one of the most important uses of outside expertise and your limited budget. I consider it money well spent and an essential part of any business model.

If your business is so small that budgetary limitations preclude paying for any HR consultants, consider becoming a member of an HR or benefit association such as the Society for Human Resource Management (SHRM) or World at Work. At a minimum, these organizations provide access to databases of HR-related information for answers to questions and suggested workplace solutions. In addition, owners and nonprofit directors can network online with other small business owners to find solutions to common problems. The annual investment of several hundred dollars is tiny compared to the value it can provide. For example, a small business owner who wants to terminate a staff member needs to do so properly and within the law or run the risk of running up a significant legal bill after the fact. Tapping these HR and benefit associations can enable business owners to comply with the law and avoid considerable harm to the business and its reputation.

Matching the HR Executive and the Culture

When I was at one of my previous companies, the CEO was looking for an executive to head HR and was very impressed by the individual in that position at Disney. The problem was that

Disney was a very progressively run company that used its HR top executive to think strate-gically. But the company I was working for was overwhelmed and its HR executive func-tioned on a catch-up, functional, transactional basis. At that company, a job came in, the job was filled, and there was no strategic role for HR. Furthermore, the CEO considered two days ahead as future planning. Had Disney's HR executive been recruited and hired, he would have been disgruntled and left within six months.

The Disney HR executive possessed an impressive resume, all the right skills, and the req-uisite experience. But recruiting and hiring someone involves finding a match. Often it takes an HR top executive to ensure that the match works effectively for both parties. I con-vinced the CEO that this HR executive wouldn't be happy and, luckily for the company, an-other executive was hired for the top HR job that was a much better fit.

Mistake 10: Hiring for Replacements Only

Just doing hiring when someone leaves a job is like putting a Band-Aid on an infection. It won't solve the problem. Compa-nies that hire in an emergency because they are desperate to fill a vacancy are likely to have someone last more than a year about 25 percent of the time.

Solution 10: Adopting a Strategic Hiring Approach

Strategic hiring, which entails figuring out your short-term and long-term needs, will double your success rate. Rather than hav-ing a revolving door of people entering and leaving, you'll find that staff will stay longer, achieve more success, and build a future for the company.

Treat hiring like any other major business decision, such as in-augurating a new marketing campaign, redefining your brand, or developing an Internet strategy. That's how you hire for the long term and succeed.

Why the Stakes Are Being Raised in Hiring

Most business leaders know that we are approaching a "perfect storm" in the workplace that has been created by global competition for human resources and the retirement of a large baby-boomer population. It's not limited access to financial capital, threat of war and famine, or even technological advancements that present the biggest threat to your organization's effectiveness and success; it's the impact of finding the right talent that may have the largest effect on an organization's growth.

If your organization is going to grow, people matter. If your organization is to innovate, people matter. If your business places customer service as one of its primary missions, people matter. If your business wants to compete globally, your people will provide your competitive edge. And yet people issues, including recruiting and retaining employees, are often put on the back burner. To realize the full potential of your organization, you need to put the right people in place and then develop them to their maximum. That requires developing a talent acquisition strategy that works, which is covered in the next chapter.

CHAPTER TWO

♦ ♦ ♦

DEVELOPING A TALENT ACQUISITION STRATEGY THAT WORKS

At most companies, the person in charge of talent acquisition is viewed as just another member of the often disrespected and belittled HR team. This talent acquisition director, who is responsible for finding, recruiting, and adopting a companywide strategy on supplying the company with the talent for the future, is another cog in the wheel. Ho-hum and no big deal. I can think of no better example of where companies go wrong in their recruiting strategy than by pointing out how they overlook and slight their director of talent acquisition. Furthermore, people who handle talent acquisition in small businesses are usually responsible for a myriad of tasks, so finding talent can also get overlooked. Small businesses would be much better off if they identified a person to specialize in finding talent, since talent is the key to helping a business grow.

My advice is to consider the talent acquisition director as equivalent to your sales director. You're probably thinking, huh? Why consider a director of talent acquisition part of the sales team? In my view, the talent acquisition head is a revenue generator. Just as your

sales team goes outside of the organization to find new customers to bring in revenue, your talent head externally recruits
talent into the organization that generates revenue. The more
skilled your talent leader, the better the employees brought into
the organization.

For example, if your company has an all-star on the sales team
that is responsible for bringing in talent responsible for 5 percent
of the company's revenue, isn't the talent director due some recognition? Without the talent leader's acumen in spotting, signing,
and recruiting talent, your company's sales would likely diminish.
Why not give the talent coordinator recognition and a piece of
sales as a reward?

Why Talent Scouts Are Worth Their Weight in Gold

An analogy in professional football underscores the point. In the
2000 National Football League (NFL) draft, the New England Patriots drafted Tom Brady on the sixth round. He was the 199th
person selected that year, so twenty-nine other NFL teams had
ample opportunities to select him but didn't. Brady had been the
second-string quarterback on the University of Michigan football
team and hadn't done well in the NFL combines, where players
are tested for speed and strength. But the head of scouting for the
Patriots saw talent in Brady and drafted him, and the quarterback
proceeded to win three Super Bowl games. Doesn't the Patriots
head of scouting deserve credit for the team's success, and by analogy, aren't corporate recruiters who bring in all-stars also worthy
of recognition and reward?

Where Most Companies Go Wrong

Two problems arise. One is that most companies don't give enough credit to their talent acquisition specialists, or in companies where there is no distinct position, they often don't pay much attention to talent acquisition. Second, most companies don't have a well-thought-out talent acquisition strategy and too often handle finding talent in a reactive way. If a person in sales leaves, HR revs up, gets itself moving, and tries to fill the position. Filling a vacant position in a stopgap way becomes the prevailing way of doing business. The last-minute approach to talent often doesn't work. The HR talent director, manager, or entrepreneur in a small business operates more like a fireman, putting out one fire and then another, but never operating strategically.

Instead, what works best is creating a deliberate, thought-out, future-oriented recruitment strategy. Companies that create a recruiting and hiring strategy for eighteen months in advance can succeed while the others that just fill vacancies in a scattershot, shotgun approach won't. **Taking steps to evaluate a company's future needs better prepares a company for any sudden changes in the marketplace.**

Creating a talent acquisition strategy for eighteen months in the future requires forethought and preplanning. Let's take the mortgage industry, which I'm familiar with because I was once the head of HR at LendingTree, a major online mortgage site, which was spun off as a separate stock, but is still owned by IAC. In 2004, the mortgage business was booming, and HR couldn't hire staff fast enough to fill vacancies. By 2008, the subprime mortgage crisis had struck, freezing hiring and then triggering downsizing of staff. What could an HR top executive and talent coordinator do in 2008 to build a strategy? The temptation would be to abandon a recruiting strategy in these tough times. The reality is that it would be smart to invest time and effort in developing a comprehensive recruiting strategy so that in eighteen months or so when the economy rebounds Lending Tree would be well positioned to pick up great talent and steal market share. Here are a few key lessons:

- *Determine your key sources of talent.* When business is booming, one thing you want to do is keep track of the key sources that are producing your most talented and qualified staff. Identify the three main sources that supplied your best people and be prepared to court them later.

- *Start building relationships early on.* The time to start reaching out to your network of sources that furnished your best applicants is when the market is sluggish, not when business is booming. In a down, sluggish market, start reaching out to the certificate programs, executive recruiters, targeted websites, MBA recruitment coordinators, and college career specialists specializing in your area. The trust that develops and the relationships that blossom over time can pay off when business picks up and your company is ready to hire.

- *Target your competitors' stars.* Moreover, start identifying the stars of your primary competitors. Attend industry functions and conferences to identify who these leaders are. Then begin "courting" them, too. I'm not suggesting you start hiring them right away. Take them out for lunch. Cultivate a relationship with them. Never ask for anything in return. But as the relationship and trust begin to develop, you are, in fact, setting the stage for attracting the best talent when your company's hiring needs demand it.

In combination, a strategy of identifying your best sources and targeting your competitors' stars will lay the groundwork for recruiting the best people in the future.

A Five-Step Program for Talent Acquisition

I've laid out a five-step program on what it takes to develop a talent acquisition strategy rather than what most organizations employ, which is the scattershot approach. The five steps are briefly defined here and then illustrated through real-life examples of three major companies.

> *Step 1: Understanding Business Cycle and Labor Market Trends*. The first thing you need to do in developing a talent acquisition strategy is to understand the entire business context. If business is booming and accountants are at a premium, your hiring strategy will have to take a certain approach. If business is plummeting and there's a glut of accountants in the market, you can take a different approach. Sizing up the marketplace is the first step to developing a hiring strategy.

> *Step 2: Getting Clear about Culture*. Every organization has its own workplace culture. What works in hiring at Microsoft, which offers a fairly structured approach to technology, may not work at Google, where creative,

open-ended thinking is revered. For that matter, what works at the U.S. Army headquarters may not work at the National Institute of Health, although both are arms of the federal government. Therefore, hiring and talent managers must recruit for their culture and not just base their selections on skills and competencies.

Step 3: Designing a Strategic Plan. Once you have sized up the marketplace and defined the culture, you need to create a strategic hiring plan. How are you going to hire? What will unify the approach? How will you involve both line managers and HR? How will you determine your hiring needs for today and a year down the road?

Step 4: Building Your Employment Brand in the Marketplace. Just as every company vies for customers against its competitors, you must compete for employees in a difficult hiring marketplace in the post-baby-boomer years. Libby Sartain, former chief HR executive at Yahoo, has said that nearly every one of the company's technical hires had received offers from Google and Microsoft. Sartain suggests HR must be able to explain why a prospective employee should choose your company over your major competitor. You need a strong three-sentence answer to offer your company's competitive edge. How a company brands itself to employees can make the difference in attracting the most talented applicants that have multiple offers to choose from.

Step 5: Developing a Sales Mentality and Rewards Program for Talent Acquisition Professionals. Like the classic Rodney Dangerfield comedic persona, talent acquisition staffs receive no respect. If they do their job right, no one notices. If vacancies aren't filled, business groups are up in arms. Treating your talent acquisition team like a sales staff by rewarding them for recruiting revenue producers is one way to grant them respect.

The Five Steps in Actual Business Practice

We interviewed Michael Cullen, the former head of EMC's global executive talent group, Libby Sartain, former chief HR officer at Yahoo, and Rocky Parker, Nationwide's associate vice president for talent acquisition, to see how these five steps play out in actual business practice. Here are examples of how these three companies implement the five steps at their respective businesses.

Step 1: Understanding Business Cycle and Labor Market Trends—How EMC Approaches Hiring Talent

EMC Corporation is a leading global IT company facing competition for talent not only from U.S.-based companies like IBM, Hewlett-Packard, and Cisco, but also prominent IT firms around the world. Michael Cullen, who once headed EMC's global executive talent office in Hopkinton, MA, said ultimately what determines EMC's hiring strategy was its business plan. "EMC's talent strategy is coupled with its strategic plan. We would discuss where we're headed in the next three years and make sure we had enough talent to fill those positions. That could change, of course, due to acquisitions and market changes. [EMC was] hiring for today and thinking about tomorrow," he said.

One of the main ingredients of EMC's talent strategy has been "hiring for the company EMC wants to become and not simply the company it is today," Cullen said. "EMC is interested as much in career progression and professional development as in filling the need of the moment."

Step 2: Getting Clear about Culture–Hiring for Cultural Fit at Yahoo and at EMC

Not only is Yahoo looking to hire staff with strong technological and innovative capabilities, but it also pursues people who fit into its culture. Yahoo's culture favors people who are bright, career-oriented, have a strong sense of purpose and what they want to accomplish, and want to grow in their job, according to Libby Sartain, former chief HR officer at Yahoo.

Like Yahoo, EMC aims to "scour the market for technical and skill fit, but also for strategic and cultural fit," Cullen noted. He described EMC's culture as attracting a "results-oriented person who is strategic in thinking and displays an ability to get the right things done with a sense of urgency." EMC screens people based on a competency model during the interview process to determine whether they display the skills that EMC seeks in its employees.

Step 3: Designing a Strategic Plan–Establishing a Talent Organization at Yahoo

When Sartain was named chief HR officer at Yahoo in 2001, she analyzed how Yahoo recruited and found talent in the past. Her initial conclusion was that Yahoo's HR hiring approach was scattershot and fragmentary. Her first major initiative was to develop Yahoo into a talent organization.

At Yahoo, there wasn't a concerted hiring strategy, just isolated efforts to try to plug a hole and fill a vacancy. Talent development wasn't emphasized, and HR didn't work closely with business managers. When HR filled a vacancy, it expected new employees to sink or swim on their own. For Yahoo to truly become a talent organization, "everyone had to be involved, the whole company, in making talent our number-one priority," Sartain said.

Sartain, who had previously been people director at Southwest Airlines, motivated the entire Yahoo leadership team to get behind the mission of making Yahoo a talent organization. Getting the buy-in and approval of the leadership team was the first step. In fact, she worked closely with both the CEO and the board of directors to gain their support. She made sure leadership was behind her efforts and was reinforcing the message that becoming a talent organization was a top priority. Furthermore, she disseminated the idea that Yahoo was a talent organization throughout the company.

After securing leadership acceptance, Sartain upgraded the HR recruiting team and organized HR recruiters around one specific Yahoo business. These HR recruiters were expected to attend meetings with business leaders and become expertly acquainted with current and future business issues.

Before launching her talent initiative, however, Sartain first took a step back and hired a consultant to assess Yahoo's hiring strengths and limitations, and she asked for recommendations to improve the current situation. The consultant interviewed a cross-section of staff members, including top executives, hiring managers and recruiters, and HR's various business partners. Sartain's goal was to ascertain where Yahoo "was and where it needed to be," she said. When the consultant evaluated Yahoo as an average talent organization, Sartain knew that rating was unacceptable for a company that wanted to operate as a leading-edge technology firm.

Having the HR recruiter become a specialist in each Yahoo business was key to achieving the goal of becoming a talent organization. In the past, managers budgeted for the workforce needs of their businesses, but it was done on an ad hoc basis. Little planning was strategic.

Under the new Yahoo talent organization, the HR recruiter for each business became responsible for Yahoo's hiring needs in that specific business for the year and started planning its future talent needs for the next few years. The recruiter, in collaboration with the business managers, evaluated the key players in each department and assessed who was likely to stay and which employees the business needed to focus in on to make sure they stayed. Then they determined the main sources of finding talent in this business and identified new sources that could be developed.

Because much of Yahoo's growth has been based on making acquisitions, future planning has to be constantly revisited. For example, Yahoo hired a consulting company that specialized in mobile communications. Impressed with the six-person business, Yahoo knew it needed to strengthen this area internally and acquired the company. What had been a weak spot in the company became an asset; the HR recruiter in each business subsequently placed hiring mobile specialists on the back burner.

Step 4: Building Your Employment Brand in the Marketplace–Creating a Hiring Competitive Edge at Yahoo and at Nationwide

In order for companies to sell their products, they must offer a competitive difference in the marketplace. In a competitive recruiting marketplace, where people with specialized technical skills are in great demand, companies have to brand their companies to attract top-flight talent. If companies don't brand their identity, they know someone else will spread the word about their company. Internet sites such as Vault.com offer insider employee surveys and feedback on how the culture really operates.

"This is the most intense marketplace in the world [in Silicon Valley]. Most everyone we hire has a competing offer from Google or Microsoft, and in technical areas, eBay and Amazon," Sartain said, though competitive pressures have eased due to the economic slowdown in late 2008. The difference maker for Yahoo is how the company brands itself and distinguishes itself from its competitors in order to appeal to the highly desirous tech talent that it seeks.

Illustrating her point is how Yahoo woos a highly desirable recruit compared to Google's approach. "People join Yahoo because they are offered specific roles. That is a differentiation," she said. When someone is offered a job at Yahoo, the person may be asked, "Do you see yourself working in Yahoo Sports or in strategic data systems?" According to Sartain, Google hires talented people and let's them find and define their own role, an approach that she describes as unstructured and unchartered compared to Yahoo's. "Yahoo solves real problems for real customers; come join us and help solve them" is the message conveyed and the brand differentiator.

Attracting talent to Nationwide, a financial services and insurance company based in Columbus, OH, involves beating out an array of competitors as diverse as Citigroup, JPMorgan Chase, Bank of America, State Farm, and Allstate. Hence, branding is very critical for them.

In his recruiting speech, Rocky Parker, Nationwide's associate vice president for talent acquisition, emphasizes Nationwide's core mission, which he describes as providing a "noble purpose, protecting the things that are most important to people—life, health, car, or home. These are things you really need to connect with to ensure the quality of your life. At Nationwide, you can make changes that have an impact on someone's life, and [it doesn't] take an act of Congress to get something done. If you have the right skills and passion, this can be a job for you," he says, emphasizing its competitive edge.

That three-sentence speech of Parker's describes Nationwide's competitive edge. It is dedicated to the customer, taps its employees' sense of community, and wants to help people while also turning a profit, a dual mission.

Step 5: Developing a Sales Mentality and Rewards Program for Talent Acquisition Professionals—Rounding Out Talent at Nationwide

At Nationwide, bringing a sales mentality to the information technology (IT) recruiting force was a very explicit goal. Rocky

Parker said of the ten IT recruiters on staff, nine of them have sales backgrounds in IT, not HR backgrounds. Because they have IT sales experience, they'll know how to identify, woo, and recruit IT specialists, and Nationwide trains them on HR tasks to round out their skills. "We bring IT recruiters in with strong sales skills and train them in HR," he concluded.

Putting the Five Steps Together into a Working Strategy

If these five steps—understanding the business cycle, defining the culture, designing a strategic plan, determining the company's brand to attract staff, and developing a sales mentality in talent acquisition—are the cornerstones of attracting talent, how does a company put them all together? How does a company avoid the trap of falling into the "someone leaves and we better find a replacement, fast" syndrome that defines the helter-skelter approach many companies have toward hiring?

As an information technology company in a very crowded field, EMC recognizes that if it is going to surmount its adversaries for talent, it needs a competitive edge, a deliberate plan, and a way to execute its strategic approach. In other words, EMC wants to stay one step ahead of a changing talent market. It does not operate in a reactive way, waiting for someone to leave and then rushing to fill a specific vacancy. Connecting its talent strategy with its future business goals helps EMC gain control over hiring.

EMC's success in finding skilled workers suggests that the stopgap approach to hiring is less effective than the more strategic, future-oriented outlook. According to Cullen, that future-oriented approach also puts emphasis on succession planning, identifying high-potential candidates, knowing their strengths, offering them stretch assignments to round out their characteristics, and figuring out who can step in to a role if the VP of marketing or finance leaves tomorrow.

Cullen's view of EMC's hard-driving culture matches feedback from EMC's current and former employees on Vault.com, the website that offers staff commentary on a company. On Vault.com, EMC's staff described its business culture as a "fast-paced work environment, an intense culture, demanding an energetic staff."

At the same time that the culture is demanding, Cullen said that EMC also emphasizes a "customers first, collaborative, and team-oriented approach." It is looking for employees that are self-reliant and capable and yet listen to others, play off of one another's ideas, and collaborate as a team.

Nor are soft-spoken, quiet people ruled out of consideration for jobs at EMC. According to Cullen, leadership comes from all personality types and profiles, not just hard-driving people. Often candidates may come across as easygoing and low-key during an interview, but when asked questions about how they've handled issues at work, their drive and passion surface. Hence, the EMC culture accommodates a variety of temperaments and backgrounds.

Why Talent Acquisition Has Changed into Talent Management: EMC Case Study

Business demands have morphed the job of talent acquisition. Today, the task is to balance pursuing talent with developing it. In a knowledge economy with millions of baby boomers retiring every year, the market for talent has been shrinking. Since it is more effective and less expensive to develop talent rather than acquire it, EMC has adjusted its talent strategy.

Hence, recruiting hones in on choosing people with certain skills that can be developed into future roles. Part of HR's job entails choosing the right training to expand employees' skills, offering the right challenges and assignments to raise experience, and therefore grooming talent to fit EMC's business needs. Developing talent can be achieved with a cross-section of staff in finance, marketing, or IT, and it is a constantly evolving process, depending on EMC's future growth plans.

Hiring for Today and Tomorrow

How can HR recruiters and their business colleagues determine, during an interview, that an applicant has the internal drive, fortitude, and skills that fit the job profile and personal attributes that EMC seeks? The HR staff asks situational and anecdotal questions to elicit how the candidate has handled similar situations in the past. For example: Tell us how you handled having multiple projects and multiple deadlines and how you managed to submit them on time. How did you devise an action plan to meet multiple deadlines? What did you do to achieve your outcomes? They are looking for specific anecdotal responses that demonstrate how the person has handled conflict, juggled multiple tasks, and collaborated with other people—namely, the skills that the company seeks in its staff.

As Cullen explained, at the same time he was seeking a candidate with the right personality that fit into EMC's culture, he was also looking to identify someone with specific competencies. That means ascertaining if the candidate has operational command of the business, has a defined set of competencies that match the level and complexity of the job, and can achieve goals with cross-functional collaboration. Candidates must show influencing skills since the employee will be working with other teams and must persuade others to get on board and work toward common goals. The goal is to find candidates with the right competencies *and* personality that fit EMC's culture.

But EMC isn't only focused on hiring someone to fill a temporary job slot for this year. It wants to hire people who can grow in their job, take the role and learn new tasks, adapt to new challenges, and be an asset to EMC for a sustained period. A middle manager in marketing, for example, may not want to be in the same job for the next five years or decade. In that event, does the person have the character to grow in the job, learn new skills, and adapt to a changing business environment? To ascertain that fact, HR asks candidates specifically where they see themselves in five or ten years. If the person has changed jobs several times and accepted new challenges in the past, that's an indicator of someone's adaptability.

Hiring Difficult-to-Fill Positions

One of the most difficult recruiting challenges for EMC has been hiring engineers. Because the United States is not producing enough engineers to meet the increasing demand, and because that demand has gone increasingly global, EMC's former CEO, Mike Ruettgers, made inroads into connecting with various educational institutions. The company funds math and science programs in local high schools in Boston and Hopkinton, MA, and sponsors another program at local colleges. Although EMC may eventually recruit a certain number of graduates of these local programs, the larger goal is to promote engineering, math, and science on the whole.

Since EMC is a global company that is competing for talent on a worldwide basis, it has also opened research and development facilities in China, India, Russia, and Israel. That approach enables EMC to hire engineers locally (overseas R&D locations do not develop talent to fill engineering vacancies in the United States, Cullen noted).

Cullen has specialized in hiring at the executive level and has become familiar with the upper echelon of talent at leading IT companies. When you've been recruiting executive IT talent for an extended period, you learn the key players at conferences, seminars, and other industry events and keep close tabs on the movement and progress of leading executives at competing IT companies. Keeping track of more junior executives at the middle manager level is much trickier and more difficult to do, Cullen suggested, because "people move so quickly these days." Hence, recruiters focus on middle managers, knowing who is out there, looking for talent at conferences, searching websites, and staying in constant discussion with targeted executive recruiters.

Developing and Acquiring Talent at Nationwide Financial Services

Like EMC in technology, Nationwide faces severe competition for talent from a wide-ranging roster of companies in its industry.

How does Nationwide, a financial services and insurance company, with competitors galore, establish a talent acquisition approach that can offer a competitive edge, woo talent, and separate
it from the crowd?

The dominant talent acquisition approach entails a "buy and
build strategy," explained Rocky Parker, Nationwide's associate
vice president for talent acquisition. This dual strategy involves
acquiring talent in the marketplace to fill openings that the organization can't supply on its own and taking people already on staff
and developing their talent. Because business and technology
changes happen quickly, sometimes acquiring the right talent is
the easiest approach to take.

For example, if Nationwide required a specialist in upgrading
its legacy technology system, a position that is hard to fill, it would
look to acquire someone in the marketplace who possesses these
skills. "There are likely only a handful of people with that expertise," Parker noted. It would be equivalent to a baseball team looking to acquire a left-handed relief specialist who could strike out
left-handers, a defined specialty.

At Nationwide, the attitude in the company is to spend "as
much time poring over people as we do financials. People are driv-
ing the business. We should make sure that as an organization we
are devoting as much credibility to people skills as we do financial
skills," Parker declared.

Nationwide is located in Columbus, OH, the fifteenth largest
city in the United States, larger than high-profile cities such as
Cincinnati, Cleveland, and Baltimore, but a city that often falls
under the radar screen and hasn't been known as a magnet to attract

talented members of Generation X and Y. Parker acknowledged that Nationwide is based "in the heart of Ohio, and that can be a challenge." Right out of college, many graduates gravitate to Miami, Seattle, New York, and Boston, but when they turn twenty-five and start getting married and raising a family, Columbus can offer more appeal. "If you really want to help others and make a great living and see your dollar stretch a long way, Nationwide's for you," he said.

Nationwide's talent approach involves building a pipeline of talented people. It attracts people via career websites, recruiting sessions at colleges, and conferences—a multipronged approach. The strategy involves looking for people with the right experience, and that experience is not necessarily limited to the financial services industry. "We seek marketing people broadly and will talk to people who have Procter & Gamble experience, for example," Parker said.

In addition to college and website recruiting, Parker added that Nationwide also pursues "the Michael Jordans of the world," so if it learns that an all-star is available, it will scoop up that talent and then find a place for the specialist in the organization. "We'll go after them even though we don't have a job, put them in a secondary role, and challenge them and develop them for future use," he stated.

Nationwide employee surveys quoted on Vault.com describe the culture as one that promotes "engaging staff," but also as "hierarchical and conservative." Parker acknowledged that as a Midwest company in the "risk aversion business," Nationwide is probably more conservative than other companies located on both coasts. Even though it has a hierarchical structure, it asks employees for feedback on all levels and responds to that feedback. For example, the company bought digital cameras for its claim adjusters based on a staff suggestion.

Hiring to Reflect a Customer Service Culture

One of Nationwide's core values is making customer service a priority. To align its values with its recruiting efforts, candidates now complete a survey of forty-eight questions on Nationwide.com to assess whether they are a good fit for a customer service organization. "We hire for attitude and train for skills," Parker said. The company is looking for people with strong relationship skills who can collaborate with others and desire to do things for others. To get a full picture of the candidate, Nationwide combines the on-line assessment with the resume (to evaluate the candidate's experience in customer service) and a behavioral-based interview, during which job candidates answer questions such as, "Tell me about a time you faced a customer service issue and how you handled it," and "What if you needed to update company policy?"

Lastly, Parker emphasized that when the company hires someone, it thinks about where the person can fit into Nationwide in the future. "What will be their next job in three year or five years? Does the person have bandwidth to grow into the next level? If they're only good for the job today, we might consider another candidate who fits better," Parker said.

Boosting the Impact of
Your Talent Acquisition Specialists

In fact, I suggest an entirely new way of treating and compensating talent acquisition professionals. Currently, they may earn

$75,000 a year on average and receive an annual merit increase of one to four percent, based on the overall performance of the organization. Why not treat them more like sales professionals than HR staff?

My recommendation is paying your talent recruiters a base salary of $45,000 to $50,000 and adding commissions based on a variety of factors. Those factors could also include retention. For example, a talent acquisition specialist might get five percent commission on a new employee's salary and an additional five percent on the employee's first-year anniversary (statistics show that the majority of new staff members who are going to leave do so in the first year). But the talent recruiter could also be paid commission on the volume of staff hired, if dealing with a call center, for example. Just as executive recruiters are often compensated based on one-third of an applicant's first-year salary and expected bonus, internal talent recruiters can be compensated based on performance.

Building a Talent Acquisition Strategy

Creating a talent acquisition strategy enables companies to win the recruiting wars, even in very competitive industries. EMC, Yahoo, and Nationwide have seasoned HR top executives who have developed cutting-edge strategies to finding talent. Although the companies operate with slight differences in their talent acquisition approaches, major themes cut across the three companies:

- ☞ All three have a strategic approach to hiring, emphasizing meeting future goals and developing people.

- They all hire for a cultural fit, not just competencies. The right person for EMC may be different than the candidate Yahoo is seeking. Even though both companies are in the IT industry, each has its own culture, and the candidate that fits for Yahoo may not blend in for EMC.

- HR must become specialists in their business, know the business as well as the operational managers, and collaborate with them on hiring and fitting employees into future business strategies.

- Succession planning is as important as filling vacancies.

- Strategic business goals drive hiring.

- Developing talent is one of the keys to retaining people and filling future slots internally.

- Making your business a talent organization and imbuing that idea throughout the company puts everyone on the same page.

- No matter what your specific business, you are in a people business and must make hiring a priority.

Creating a Team Approach to Hiring

Someone once said it takes a village to raise a child. In this case, it takes a collaborative team approach to build a talent acquisitions approach. The HR top executive, the HR talent coordinator, or the operational manager in a small business responsible for hiring meets with senior business leaders. The issues to explore: What are our key business initiatives for the next year to eighteen months?

What new business are we exploring? What overseas expansion, if any, is planned? Where do we see baby boomers retiring or turnover likely? What do our exit interviews reveal about turnover? Based on the feedback from business managers, the HR talent coordinator develops a strategic labor forecast for the future that addresses issues such as, What are our most significant needs down the road? Where are the gaps? Where will we have to step up hiring? Will we need sales, marketing, financial, and new product staff?

At Yahoo, becoming future-oriented in hiring required an entirely new approach. Workforce planning became an emphasis rather than afterthought. HR staff did extensive succession planning, focusing in who the number-two and number-three people were in the organization and who could replace the leader if the head of the department left. "When Yahoo did this the first or second year, their bench was empty," Sartain revealed. By focusing on workforce planning, Yahoo strengthened its team and developed two or three key people who could move into the head position. Workforce planning enabled Yahoo to develop a stronger team with more seasoned and experienced people.

Recruiting the Hardest-to-Fill Roles

Despite its brand differentiation, Yahoo, like other tech companies, has a hard time filling certain roles. For example, algorithmic search scientists, data gurus, and certain economists are in such demand that they are very difficult to recruit.

What does Yahoo do? Once it identifies this talent, it actively develops a rapport with them. For example, it has recruiters who read articles in academic and technical journals specializing in algorithmic search, and who then go to college campuses, attend conferences, and seek out entrepreneurs. Establishing a relationship with these specialists leads to courting them, wooing them, and, when the match is right, offering them a position. Sartain stresses that Yahoo's main selling points are its brand identity, how it solves major Internet problems, that it reaches one of the widest audiences on the Internet, and that its staff is passionate.

By analogy, it would be like the director of personnel or military recruitment for the armed forces meeting with the head of the Joint Chiefs of Staff to determine our nation's major trouble spots in the next year. Will we likely need forces in Iran, Afghanistan, Bosnia, or Iraq? Will the 120,000 troops suffice, or will we require more soldiers? Just as businesses develop labor forecasts, military personnel design troop forecasts.

Social Networking Sites Are Spreading the Word

Even social networking sites are having a major impact on employee branding and recruiting, Sartain said. Before the Microsoft takeover bid occurred, Yahoo downsized some staff. Within hours of the downsizing being announced, messages by the Yahoo employees affected were sent on Facebook and Twitter. The staff that was being dismissed was writing e-mails and instant messages, almost as the downsizing was happening, saying they had just gone into HR, were discussing severance, and would be posting their resumes later that afternoon. By day's end, people on these social networking sites, not to mention Yahoo's competitors, knew who was laid off and could request their resumes if they so desired. "The whole marketplace for looking for work has changed. The talent marketplace is as demanding as the customer marketplace. You need to market to your people just as you do to your customers," Sartain said.

One comment from a hiring manager years ago still resonates for Sartain. When a vacancy arose, the HR recruiter asked the hiring manager if he knew anyone he'd like to recommend for the job. "If I knew someone, why do I need you?" the hiring manager replied. At that moment, Sartain knew that HR would have to play a much more active role in recruiting that involved a deeper knowledge of talent and the business to add value and stay one step ahead of the curve.

A New Hiring Paradigm

In this new paradigm, the entire process of finding talent has changed and been overhauled. No longer does HR function in a limited way. It is now an active part of a dynamic hiring process. This new way of hiring considers both short-term and long-term needs. HR must therefore be involved in business meetings, strategic planning, and business projections to anticipate the organization's future employment needs.

For example, a technology firm was in negotiations for a multiyear partnership with Google. At the same time, an HR person at the technology company was targeting Google to recruit a replacement, which could lead to conflict and potentially ruin the multimillion-dollar partnership. Had HR been involved in all of its company's business dealings, it would have been aware of the partnership discussions and would not have targeted the Google employee.

In this new environment, HR staff creates a strategic hiring blueprint. Rather than just act as a service that fills a job when an opening arises, the skilled HR person is in constant touch with business management. The HR professional works in concert with the business, reviewing job descriptions, seeing how the needs of the organization are changing, and aligning with changing business needs. For HR specialists to do a good job, they must be knowledgeable about the business, see issues from the business manager's viewpoint, and understand the revenue imperatives as well as the long-term goals of the business.

Furthermore, the HR manager and the staff must understand the needs of the manager. What kind of person will work best with the hiring manager? Is the business seeking a collaborative team player or a self-initiator?

In addition, the HR person must know the inner workings of the business. What makes an Internet start-up successful? What kind of auditors succeed at PricewaterhouseCoopers or any of the Big Four firms in a new world of scrutiny and reliance on ethics? What kind of editors will thrive in a world where the Internet is gaining momentum over traditional publishing?

What the Talent Coordinator Does

HR consists of many people with different specialties. There are HR experts in employee relations, benefits experts, and talent acquisition specialists. There's another expert who is referred to as the HR generalist who functions like a general practitioner and covers every area of HR.

In recruiting, the HR staff that specializes in talent acquisition plays the most important role. One of the main tasks necessary involves continuous networking to constantly assess the talent marketplace. It is their responsibility to keep track and stay abreast of talent in several areas (depending on how HR is structured)—for example, marketing, finance, design, editing, and all the crucial roles that have to be filled. In larger companies, there may be HR recruiters who specialize only in hiring attorneys, IT technical specialists, or editors.

In many ways, talent coordinators or recruiters operate like casting directors in the film business. Casting directors must keep tabs on the best talent available so that when a film is being cast they can provide the director with the best candidates to audition or interview and let the director make the choice.

For talent specialists to do their job expertly, they must work with business line managers in charge of each area. Each department must identify exactly what its needs are today, two years from now, and five years in the future. HR, in consultation with each department head in a large business, or the owner in a small business, or the executive director in a not-for-profit or governmental agency, must have a running list of every job and a full-fledged job description that is updated annually, and they must maintain a constant overview of who is available inside and outside the organization.

Why Hiring Will Provide the
Competitive Edge in the Future

In the next ten years, the companies that solve their people and hiring issues will prevail as winners and those that don't will fall by the wayside. Whether these problems are solved by HR, outsourcers, consultants, or managers themselves is secondary to the fact that choosing the right people will lead to success and failing to do so will lead to failure.

In my experience, hiring and retaining the best people is difficult and becoming more complex by the day. It is also not a luxury—it's not simply an add-on or extra responsibility that one can get around to when there's free time. Whether you are management for a Fortune 500 company, one of the millions of small businesses that fuel the American economy, an arm of our vast and critical local, state, and federal government, or a not-for-profit association, getting your talent right is critical. Unless your organization is staffed by robotics, you cannot accomplish anything without people. And if you do not have a well-oiled machine in place to identify the best people, recruit them, and retain them, your organization is quite likely to fail.

In a Knowledge Economy, the
New Hiring Approach Is a Necessity

Times have changed. There was a time not long ago when you could hire nearly anyone and train that person to do what you needed to get done. This is how things worked when our economy was primarily a manufacturing one. The last decade, however, has brought us into a full-fledged knowledge economy, which requires a totally different type of highly trained, smarter worker. This new breed of worker is harder to find and harder to please.

Attracting talent is about *retaining* today's knowledge workers—not just finding them.

When you talk to most savvy business people about their recruiting and hiring needs eighteen months into the future, they look at you dumbfounded. Eighteen months in the future for most people and you might as well be talking about eighteen years in the future. Most business people spend their days putting out fires for today. They are mired in the present, focused on quarterly earnings, responding to any daily initiative that the CEO, SVP, or senior manager conveys to them. And in small businesses, where everyone is doing multiple jobs, looking into the future is a luxury that few have time for. How then can a company build a strategy for finding talent and then retaining that talent? How do you make your employees fall in love with your company? That's what we'll cover in chapter 3.

CHAPTER THREE

◆ ◆ ◆

RETAINING PEOPLE BY MAKING THEM FALL IN LOVE WITH THE COMPANY

One of the mandates for Sheryl Sandberg, named chief operating officer of Facebook at the beginning of 2008, was to build a larger organization at the social networking site. Since she helped formulate a recruiting and staffing policy at Google in her previous job, Sandberg knew what she was doing. Soon after joining Facebook, Sandberg instituted a series of guidelines covering employee performance reviews, identifying and recruiting new employees, and introducing management-training programs. From the outset, her focus was on creating an HR policy and staffing outlook that would enable the organization to hire the right people and grow while maintaining its core culture.

Since Facebook only had 550 employees and was going to expand rapidly, Sandberg knew the organization was facing a transformational period. "Scaling up is hard," she told staff, according to *The Wall Street Journal*, "and it's not as much fun not to know everyone you work with. But if we get to work on things that affect hundreds of millions of people instead of tens of millions, that's a trade-off worth making."

Sandberg built an organization at Facebook with a hiring approach that aimed to engender loyalty in staff by creating a dynamic culture and a successful company that people don't want to leave. Hiring the best talent—and keeping them—requires a strategic approach to long-term employment.

Avoiding the Stopgap, Shotgun Approach

Despite all the lip service given that people are our most important asset, hiring a new employee is often done using what I like to call the stopgap approach. Stopgap means plug the leak as quickly as possible. Get the resumes, see who fits the job, interview, and hire. Furthermore, the process is often conducted in a shotgun—not just stopgap—manner. That's the reality of hiring when every senior executive and hiring manager is putting out fires, dealing with the latest corporate initiative, trying to make their numbers, and then has to also identify the right candidate.

To get you to focus on long-term hiring, I'll offer some tips on hiring and retention and then provide four steps to getting employees to fall in love with the company, which is the key to keeping them. I'll discuss practices that cutting-edge employers can invoke to inspire retaining talented employees and describe what it takes to becoming an employee-centered organization. Finally, Beverly Carmichael, the chief people officer at Ticketmaster and formerly at Southwest Airlines, will demonstrate how employing many of these techniques keeps skilled employees satisfied and retained for as long as possible.

The Cost of Losing Employees

A 2008 article in *HR Management* magazine noted that replacing a worker costs on average 100 percent to 125 percent of an employee's annual salary. If an employee earned $75,000 a year, replacing that person sets the employer back $75,000 to $100,000, once you calculate the executive recruiter fees and the cost of advertising and training. Moreover, the employer loses productivity and often suffers a decline in morale as colleagues wonder why they are staying and whether the grass is more appealing elsewhere. And yet many organizations still ignore employee retention.

Retaining People Isn't About Twenty-Five Years Anymore

A generation ago, organizations believed they could keep an employee for twenty-five years or more. About a decade ago, employers looked to retain people for ten years or more. Now people recognize that many talented, young employees, right out of college or coming in with their MBA, are going to stay no more than three to five years before moving on. If you keep them for three to five years, you are making a very good return on your recruiting investment. Any time spent at the organization less than that and you've lost money.

Why then are you going to inject lots of money and time into training and development programs? You are looking to retain your stars. To use a baseball analogy, major league teams spend millions of dollars on their minor league programs, hoping to find the next Alex Rodriguez or one or two All-Stars who will stay with the team for several years. If teams find two All-Stars a year, the money spent will have been worthwhile. Furthermore, since many baseball players are free agents who move from team to team, finding the highest bidder for their services, many teams can't afford to hold on to stars for more than five years. Corporate America could learn a lesson or two from baseball; they have to invest money into training to keep their future leaders.

In short, you are investing your recruiting money in finding stars, knowing the bulk of your trainees and new hires will leave in five to ten years. Yes, every employee is critical, but reality says they won't be waiting around for a gold watch after twenty-five years. If you can keep your All-Stars for the long term, your organization will prosper. Once you identify future leaders, you can do everything in your power to retain them.

Most other employees, who aren't your future leaders, are inevitably going to leave to find greener pastures. After three to five years at the same job, most people are going to get stale. What you need to do is move them out of one division into another, if you want to keep and groom them, or let them leave. Hence, some turnover is healthy. You want a natural flow of people moving into the organization who bring new skills, and employees moving out of the organization who may want to switch careers or transition into new challenges, or whose performance reviews suggest that they are not your highly motivated and skilled employees.

You Need Workplace Stability, but You Don't Need Stagnation

Of course, you want to keep your stars and most skilled people— your engineers, software developers, marketing whizzes, and communication gurus. But turnover is inevitable and necessary. While you want workplace stability, you want some of your mid-level performers to find new opportunities that inspire them. How many years can you work at a call center before burning out? You don't want your employees to become burned out or cynical, or to reach a point where they are just going through the motions.

Ask most hiring managers to consider choosing the right candidate for the long term and they'll look at you bewildered and flustered, as if you just announced that you saw an alien in an unidentified flying object in your backyard. For most managers who are under the gun and juggling multiple tasks, long-term hiring often entails choosing someone who will be on board next week or maybe the next quarter. Many HR specialists and business managers just don't have the time to think about whether the employee is likely to stick around for the next few years or leave six months after starting the job. All they want to do is fill the vacancy now.

Developing a New Mindset about Hiring and Retention

Retaining a greater number of employees requires an entirely new mindset for most executives, HR people, and senior managers. Companies can legally terminate an employee at will, and most top executives (including HR executives) have come to believe that they are calling the shots. Ten years ago, when baby boomers dominated the market and there were many more employees than openings, this outlook may have been true. In a knowledge economy, when many specialists are in demand, employees exert power as well. In short, business executives, entrepreneurs, military leaders, and heads of nonprofits must strive to become service leaders and win over the hearts and souls of their employees.

Changing an organization's outlook toward keeping employees requires reframing. You'll have to stop viewing employees as interchangeable parts, which may (or may not) have worked when factory workers could be replaced on production lines. Nowadays, even auto assembly line workers require advanced computer and technological skills.

Here are five distinct approaches to retaining employees: (1) make retaining employees a priority, (2) adopt a clear approach to hiring for the long term, (3) create an employee-centered culture to hold on to employers, (4) become a cutting-edge company in retention (just as you are in product development) to provide your competitive edge, and (5) master the secrets to getting employees to fall in love with the company.

Hiring for the Long Term

The shotgun approach to hiring doesn't work long term. You need to rethink how you approach hiring and whether you are choosing people who will stay or are just making a temporary stop to strengthen a resume.

Hiring for the long term doesn't have to entail looking at hundreds of resumes, interviewing a dozen candidates, and spending two weeks that you don't have on an intensive job search. Here are some approaches to choosing the right candidate for the long haul:

☞ *Let the detailed job description dictate the choice.* The more you hire for both skill and attitude, the easier time you will have finding the right person. Most hiring managers go wrong because they turn the search into a subjective decision and they start looking for the candidate who most reminds them of themselves. If you stick with one criterion—who best fills the job—it will guide you to the right person.

☞ *Ask the right questions.* Which candidate has best handled these conflicts before? What in the candidate's past proves that he or she can handle the job? What anecdotes reveal that the person is best suited for the position? Too many interviewers ask the obvious, yes or no questions, and they end up eliciting little information from the candidate. Asking the right questions will guide the hiring decision.

☞ *Think about the future, not just today.* It's not always about choosing the person with the right skills, but who has the right skills and will last in the job for several years. If the candidate has the perfect background but shows signs of wanting to be promoted overnight or jump at the first offer six months later, hire someone else. Will this candidate prosper in this job over the next three to five years? If the answer is yes, you may have a good fit.

☞ *Be straight about the job.* Don't say that the job is on commission and bonuses will start immediately, if bonuses will only begin when revenue numbers are hit, which could take six months. If you say misleading things about the job, the hours, the demands, salary, or bonuses, expect fast departures.

Developing a Hiring Competitive Edge

Staying one step ahead of the competition is a requirement these days. But business leaders forget that keeping an edge in choosing the right staff is as important as updating your product line.

Most sales and marketing executives know exactly what the strengths and limitations of their competitor's products are. Just as Sprint, Verizon, or T-Mobile salespeople know every detail of their competitors' plans and can explain why theirs is better, talent recruiters should know what their competitors are offering and be able to counter their strengths. If you are a talent acquisition specialist at Microsoft, you better know what Google and Yahoo are doing to attract staff and have a competitive edge ready to present. Hypothetically, a Google recruiter knows what Microsoft offers in developmental training and healthcare and can explain why Google's training and medical plans are superior.

Furthermore, the larger the organization gets, the more difficult it often is to retain staff. A March 26, 2008, *Forbes* article written by Wendy Tanaka noted how Google had lost its director of social media, chief financial officer, and top engineers to Facebook. Google had been stealing employees from Microsoft, and now Facebook was raiding Google. "Now Google is big—16,800 people at last count. Internally, a few people have been heard to grumble that the company might just be a bit too big," Tanaka wrote. Facebook only has 1,000 employees and limited bureaucracy and can offer a more personalized environment and more room to grow.

The article noted that "workers who don't move around risk getting labeled as stagnant." The tech world is foreshadowing other industries, where moving from job to job reveals your desirability in the marketplace while staying at a firm suggests an inability to take risks and may mark you as someone who is getting stale, losing one's drive, and avoiding new challenges.

One of the most effective ways to stem employee departure is to encourage your staff to fall in love with the company. The better you treat employees and the more attentive your managers are to them, the stronger the odds that you can retain employees, rather than lose them to your competitor.

Developing Camaraderie and Esprit de Corps

There are several ways to encourage your staff to fall in love with the company. One way to build employee loyalty is to develop esprit de corps. We are all in this together, and we're a team like the Dodgers or Red Sox. Sometimes T-shirts and caps can make people feel like they are part of a team with pride in their company. As a team, they can take on all competitors. A little employee branding can go a long way to building esprit de corps.

Stressing social engagements that aren't work related also can build teamwork. I've taken my staff out bowling to foster camaraderie. I'll mix up the teams and put people on teams who don't work together or may not have gotten along in the past. But when four members of a team are vying for a $250 gift certificate for the best scores, and one team member puts two strikes together in a row, the high-fives between them start flying. Furthermore, taking the staff to lunch, outside of the pressures of the office, also builds camaraderie.

Most managers think the best and easiest way to motivate an employee is through a salary raise. But a $2,000 or $3,000 increase, after taxes, fades fast. I prefer bestowing more personalized gifts that offer more recognition. For example, the son of one of my staff members is on a middle school basketball team. When the Harlem Globetrotters were in town, I was able to secure four tickets to a box suite and offered it to her, her husband, and two kids. Those kids will remember attending that game forever, and my employee will remember that night for a long time to come. Making your employees feel special helps them fall in love with the company.

Sometimes you need to recognize employees and their families. When we were launching RushmoreDrive.com, the staff was working twelve to fourteen hours a day and spending less time with their spouses. After the new business debuted, I planned a weekend for the twenty or so staff members and their spouses or partners at a nearby inn. The entire weekend cost little more than $10,000 for two nights' lodging and several meals, but I think the payback in loyalty to the company will transcend the dollars spent.

Making Everyone Feel Special and Going Out of Your Way for Your All-Stars

Most organizations go wrong when they forget that people make the organization. It's people who manufacture, market, and sell the products. And every single person in the organization plays a role. Alex Rodriguez may have been Most Valuable Player of the American League, but for the New York Yankees to win a World Series, twenty-five guys have to perform well. And that goes for the second-string catcher and the relief pitcher who comes in for one inning, not just Rodriguez.

Still, it's perfectly acceptable to go out of your way for your All-Stars. Giving them tickets to a professional basketball game or assigning them to a one-week leadership program at the well-respected Aspen Institute, for example, motivates them and encourages them to stay.

Four Steps for Making Your Employees Fall in Love with the Company

Step 1: Reward people fairly and in line with the marketplace.

Step 2: Treat staff well; focus on recognizing every employee's contributions.

Step 3: Train employees and improve skills on their current job.

Step 4: Develop your most talented employees whom you think have leadership potential.

Step 1: Reward People Fairly

If you think you can pay people below industry levels and retain them, you're mistaken. Once you decide to pay them a competitive salary, most people aren't going to leave unless they get a 20 percent increase.

When most companies think of compensating people, they think salary. The job offers $60,000 a year, and that's the figure that most companies emphasize in order to lure an employee. What's needed to retain people is a much broader view of compensation. Annual income should serve as the starting point since most organizations pay in the same range and don't vary much. Going beyond salary, you'll need to create a competitive edge in hiring for your organization, just as you do with your products or services.

For example, some companies now offer free on-site childcare centers. A mother on staff can now visit her child at lunchtime and know that her kid is receiving excellent care. How much is that worth to a parent? The kind of comfort that daycare for their child at work offers a parent transcends dollars and cents and can be a major factor in retaining an employee. Furthermore, these perquisites heighten retention by offering a competitive edge. Employees considering another job offer would think twice if the competitor didn't offer a childcare center.

Step 2: Treat Staff Well

In his much-read book *The Tipping Point*, Malcolm Gladwell introduced "the stickiness factor" as a way to authentically and personally reach an employee. He suggests that to retain employees, you must know them, create a singular point of view, and devise a message that resonates to keep them. When I use the term *stickiness*, I'm recommending that HR executives and business managers create a personalized message that reaches every employee and encourages them to stay. Jack Welch liked Gladwell's "stickiness" idea so much that he used it as a recurring theme in his best seller, *Winning.*

To raise your "stickiness" factor and boost your employee retention, ask yourself if you know the motivation of each member of your staff. Being able to leave at five o'clock to see their child play in a soccer match may work for some employees, but it may not work for another employee who wants two extra days of vacation to travel to Alaska. One employee wants to be sent to the Aspen Institute to gain leadership skills while another one wants special technology training to keep up-to-date with peers.

The more you can personalize and customize your retention strategy, the more chance you'll have of keeping your top employees. Obviously, if your organization has 131,000 employees, you can't devise 131,000 different retention programs, but you can do your best to reach all employees through their managers. The more your HR and senior managers can personalize strategies to reach each employee, the stronger your retention will be and the more you will have enhanced the "stickiness" factor with your staff.

Creating a Culture of Fun

People want to make as much money as possible, but they also want to work in an atmosphere that is positive, reinforcing, and where they're not belittled or censured. Creating a culture where bosses treat their staff with respect, challenge them, and establish a fun environment, despite working hard, leads to retaining employees. Yelling at employees, micromanaging them, criticizing and humiliating them, lying to them, and not recognizing them for their efforts are all behaviors that will lead to employees running for the exit and resigning for other opportunities.

When Southwest Airlines was just getting off the ground (literally and figuratively) and challenging American, United, Continental, and Delta, its employees were known for working longer hours than the competitors. And yet, at the same time, Southwest had the lowest turnover and highest retention rate in the industry.

Herb Kelleher, founder and CEO of Southwest Airlines and still its chairman, created an atmosphere of having fun on the job. He hired only employees whom HR considered gregarious, outgoing, and flexible. And then he made sure that they had fun on the job. Southwest sent each employee a birthday card. That simple gesture sent a message that every employee was special. Kelleher dressed up in costumes on Halloween and sometimes just on average days, injecting fun and unpredictability on the job. His point: No day was routine at Southwest. And though Southwest employees worked hard, they enjoyed themselves and didn't want to leave.

What Kelleher mastered at Southwest was the simple idea that employees want to be recognized for their efforts and prefer to work in an upbeat, supportive environment, not a hostile, demeaning one. Nor did any of what Southwest and its managers did cost much money. Sending a birthday card to every employee was cheap but effective. Organizing Halloween parties for the staff was inexpensive. The attitude that pervaded the company was that we're all in this together, the CEO and CFO, pilots, flight attendants, and baggage handlers all contributed to making this airline special.

You don't have to be a Fortune 500 company or even a public company to devise innovative ways to retain employees. Kevin Trapani, the CEO of the Redwoods Group, an insurance provider with 110 employees, based in Morrisville, NC, lost about 10 percent of his staff in one year to his competitors who offered them raises that he couldn't match. For a small firm, losing a dozen employees damages productivity and morale.

Trapani devised an idea that worked for most of his employees, which Malcolm Gladwell would have deemed the stickiness factor. Since many of his employees had children and tuition at North Carolina's state universities was rising above inflation, Trapani offered each employee a free year of public college education for their offspring. In 2003, when he established the perquisite, college cost $5,000 a year at a state school, which subsequently rose to $6,000 a year. Every Redwoods Group employee who had been with the firm for two years was eligible. Every employee now receives a $6,000 stipend if their child attends a North Carolina state school.

The result of Trapani's free college idea was that turnover was cut from a dozen employees leaving to two a year. Furthermore, this policy has enabled him to attract better employees who are motivated by an employer who cares about the staff and their families.

Step 3: Train Employees and Improve Skills

Many new hires joining a firm are smart and educated but have no real skill sets. Training enhances and improves their current skills. What the organization is reaping from these new hires is a new approach to doing business and a keen knowledge of the most contemporary trends. If you want to learn what makes Generation Y tick, the role that social networking plays, and how people make choices on the Internet, odds are the recent graduate can offer a fresh perspective. In return for bringing in this new talent, organizations train new employees. The relationship is symbiotic in that both gain: The new hires improve their skills and the organization reaps three to five years of its new employees' insights and recent education.

There's nothing mysterious about what kind of training works best. Training that makes you better at the job you are doing today, enhances your current skills, and makes you more effective and efficient constitutes good training.

The kind of training that works best for each person differs from employee to employee. Some staff members work best at online learning while others recoil from it and prefer old-fashioned, classroom interaction. Again, knowing each of your employees is key to producing the best possible training.

Effective training produces a win-win outcome. Employees gain because they are learning new skills. The learning process motivates them and encourages them to stay longer on the job. And the organization gains because the staff member is going to be more efficacious on the job (a topic explored in more detail in chapter 5).

Step 4: Develop Your Most Talented Employees

Training and development are different. Training is about teaching one to do the job he or she has today. Development focuses on preparing one to perform a broader role in the future. Training is usually about gaining specific tactical skills. Development is all about preparing leaders. Harry can be a widget maker, but does he have the right potential to train others to manufacturer widgets and lead the company? If he does, the organization invests in his professional development.

On what basis do you identify future leaders? That's what managing is all about. In basketball, scouts detected early on that LeBron James had the right talents to become arguably the best player of his generation. Just as scouts identify talent on the basketball court, so do managers in business.

Avoiding favoritism and not just selecting people who are mirror images of you are the cornerstones of effective management. When I was an HR executive at Viacom, I took a leadership development course in diversity—and it wasn't about the usual forms of diversity. Instead of concentrating on race and gender, the course zeroed in on recognizing the talents of people who are different from you. We were taught to look for leadership characteristics in less gregarious and demonstrative employees. Identifying that talent is the bailiwick of the skilled manager.

Why Do So Many Employees Leave in the First Year?

Many organizations operate like a twenty-one-year-old guy on a first date who spends lots of time wooing someone into having dinner with him and then, having won over his date, loses interest. You create a dynamic portrait of the organization, tout its strengths, talk about opportunities, and then after the person is hired, you forget about him. You move on to your priorities and forget about your newest employee, who is left to sink or swim. Left to their own devices without supervision or guidance, most new employees sink, lose interest, and jump at the first chance to find a boss who will groom them and an organization that pays attention to them.

Failure to develop staff is a major reason people leave their first year. In addition, there's often a bad cultural or business fit. Often, when people interview for a job, the company's overarching strategy isn't communicated. If a company hires a new IT designer and soon after the company announces a 10 percent layoff and backing off from new projects, the recent hire, whose project has been delayed, could easily get disillusioned. Furthermore, middle-to higher-level staff members receive stock or vesting options only if they stay three to five years on the job, depending on the contract. If employees are unhappy, rather than suffer through three years, they will opt out fast and start fresh on a new job.

The best way to minimize staff departures in that all-important first year is to be as clear as possible about what the new hire will do that first year and possibly the second year. Focusing on the cultural fit between new hire and job description will minimize departures.

It's Not Customer Service; It's Employee Service

Ignoring employee retention is like an organization gaining a million-dollar contract and not servicing the customer. If a company gains a contract and then doesn't deliver customer service, it will lose the account. Similarly, if an organization recruits and woos top employees and then pays little or no attention to them, doesn't train them, groom them, or consider their career growth, those people will walk and you've lost them. It underscores how organizations need to treat people decisions and employee satisfaction with the same importance and consideration as business decisions. If not, your turnover rate will rise and you'll keep losing top employees to your competitors.

Yet most companies shortchange their employees and don't spend nearly enough time on meeting their employees' needs as they do their customers' needs. The more you can retain employees (the ones you want to keep), the better your customer service will be, since more experienced employees tend to deliver superior service. Retain your employees, reduce recruiting costs, and improve your bottom line. It's a win-win-win.

What Cutting-Edge Organizations Do When
Hiring for the Long Term

Here are some practices that cutting-edge companies put into action to inspire and retain talented employees.

1.   Leading organizations hire for the long term; they don't just fill a vacancy. They consider whether the employee is likely to stay for several years and build that goal into the whole hiring process.

2.   Leaders are straight with employees. They don't withhold information about the job. They present job details straightforwardly and try to connect the future employee with the job qualifications.

3.   Leaders base their hiring selection on objective criteria, not on which candidate will please the boss the most, acts like the hiring managers, or agrees with most of the hirer's views.

4.   Breakthrough organizations focus on their newly hired employees. How can we best groom them? What mentors will help them grow? What training will motivate them? What job do we see the employee in next, and how can we help the person move there? Retaining is as important as hiring.

5.   Cutting-edge organizations charge every manager with getting to know their employees. What motivates them? What drives them? What will make them stay? Managers must stay as attuned to employees as they do to their product lines and customers. Managers are then compensated on their ability to groom, train, and develop staff.

6.   Managers perform spot-checks with their employees, holding open-ended dialogues that allow the employee to

reveal what's really going on. Is the employee satisfied? Is the job living up to expectations? These conversations must take place during the first six months, since that's often a turning point when employees lose their edge and begin to consider finding a new position.

How the Power Shift Has Changed

Hiring for the long term is necessary in many fields because the number of knowledge workers can't meet the demand. A March 13, 2008, *BusinessWeek* article noted that Siemens, the international engineering and construction behemoth, had to curtail some of its activities in Germany because it couldn't hire enough engineers to oversee some of its projects. When there are fewer knowledge workers around than companies can hire, employees wield as much power as the employers. Yet some companies still operate as if they exert the control over hiring.

In most hiring these days, job applicants question recruiters as much as HR staff interrogates them. Applicants have read Vault.com and other websites; they know what current and former employees say about your culture and question promises that won't be maintained or are exaggerated. Most employees recognize that they are not going to spend twenty-five years at one company earning a gold watch; they are more likely to operate like free agents in sports who move from team to team. Consequently, many in-demand employees hold as much power as the organization does.

While many people focus on salary as the key driver of what attracts a person to a company, often it's not the telltale decider. Most job seekers who compare salaries discover that most companies offer the same basic salary within a 5 percent range. Once hired, most people won't leave for a 5 percent or even 10 percent hike, which after taxes becomes almost indistinguishable.

Focusing on the Intangibles to Retain Employees, Not Just Salary

What keeps people at a company are the intangibles. Is my boss reasonable, and am I recognized and respected by the boss? Does my work challenge me, and am I learning new skills? Is there a chance for advancement? Do my values and the organization's mission match? Does the company treat people well? Are we a growing or declining company? Am I motivated to help the company reach its goals? Is the organization ethical? Is it involved in the community? Do I get along with my colleagues?

Most people leave because of the boss. It's true. Most people change jobs, not because they are seeking more money, but because of dissatisfaction with their bosses. According to Fredric Frank, CEO of TalentKeepers, a Maitland, FL-based consulting company that specializes in employee retention, "You don't leave a job; you leave a boss." If the boss isn't skilled at building trust or developing a climate that challenges and supports people, employees leave.

You can therefore boost retention levels by training and strengthening the skills of your managers. Train every manager and expect them to get to know what makes their employees tick, what sustains them over the long haul, and what will challenge them in the future, and your retention level will rise.

The best leadership training provides managers with the skills to deal more effectively with their staff. Courses that help managers learn what motivates each employee, with techniques on how to reach each employee, offer the most effective training. Dealing with difficult employees and turning them around is another essential skill. The more skills your managers have in their toolkit, the better able they will be to reach employees and help keep them motivated.

In my view, when managers know what motivates each employee, they have it made. Some employees are motivated solely by money; others crave attention. For some employees, you should concentrate on providing recognition and the spotlight, whereas the more mercenary employees want to see extra income.

Lessons Learned from a Financial Services Leader

Where other financial services companies have faltered and lost millions of dollars in the subprime mortgage and credit crisis, Goldman Sachs has stood above the herd. What is its secret? The 2007 Goldman Sachs annual report stated that "ultimately, our success depends on the quality of the people we attract and *retain*." Its secret in pursuing talent is involving its entire staff, not just HR, in the recruiting process. As the firm noted, "Everyone from our junior to our most senior people commits time and focus to our recruiting efforts."

But its efforts don't stop in its highly organized recruiting efforts. Once the staff member is hired and on board, intensive training begins. Goldman Sachs offers 2,400 online and classroom courses that involve more than 90 percent of its staff. Training amounts to 950,000 hours of staff time, showing the company's dedication to development and retention. Moreover, the firm promotes variegated and challenging assignments that also heighten retention.

Introducing Stay Interviews

Too many organizations use the "sink or swim" philosophy. Once employees are hired, the organization pays little attention to them until they want to leave. Many organizations learn that employees are dissatisfied during an exit interview. Waiting to find out what makes your employees tick at an exit interview is too late and after the fact.

Instead, conduct "stay" interviews. Find out what drives each employee, which will translate into what will make the employee stay. In addition, ascertain what the employee likes and doesn't like about the company. What motivates the employee? Is it working on new projects? Receiving more training? Speaking at conferences? Too often managers are so focused on financial goals or lack the necessary communication skills that they don't ask employees what drives them and therefore don't know what will keep employees— until it's too late. You need to know what makes people stay at your organization.

On the other hand, exit interviews can also help provide valuable information to help retain employees. First thing I recommend is to outsource exit interviews to a consulting firm. Most employees are reluctant to burn bridges and will never reveal to an insider in HR why they are really leaving. Granted confidentiality, more employees will divulge more honest responses to a third party not aligned with the company.

The most important takeaway from exit interviews is to elicit information from the employee and then act on it. For example, when I was head of HR at Paramount, we saw a pattern of several people leaving one department. Most departing employees said they felt trapped because their boss said she was going to be there for the next ten years and told her staff there was no room to advance. Not surprisingly, one by one, her subordinates gravitated out of the department, and often to competitors.

Working with Managers to Devise Creative Solutions to Keep Staff

Working with this Paramount manager and explaining why we were trying to prevent talented people from leaving, we devised a rotation approach. We created four specialties within her department and shifted people around to expand their skills. In that way, we could rotate people with assignments over five years, keeping them much longer than we did in the past. We still lost some people but managed to reduce turnover.

Finding the right people is critical to your organization's success, but losing good staff exerts too high a price on most company's health and well-being. If your turnover rate is high and talented people are leaving at regular intervals, your company's future is compromised. On the other hand, you can keep a much higher percentage of your employees by taking steps to become an employee-centered organization (as discussed later in this chapter).

Grooming Leaders

Many companies describe future leaders as high-potential people. What happened to me when I was an attorney in 1993 at Blockbuster, then owned by Viacom, serves as a prototype for how you develop high-potential people.

I had graduated from law school at age twenty-three, had sterling credentials, and by 1995, had proved myself as a capable lawyer in labor employment. My boss, Tom Hawkins, the general counsel at Blockbuster, identified me as a high-potential candidate and mentored me. He told me that he was only a few years older than me and wasn't leaving his position any time soon. He asked me where I saw myself in my career five or ten years down the road. Did I want to move up as an attorney and become general counsel, or transfer into HR, or move into a business line? I told him that HR offered the most opportunity for me.

Hawkins then introduced me to Blockbuster's head of HR. He told the HR top executive that I possessed labor law expertise, and asked if I could sit in on some HR meetings to learn more about the area. In addition, he arranged for me to take a variety of developmental courses that would train me to become a manager. He set me on a path that led me to where I am today.

I try to emulate Tom Hawkins's approach to mentoring my best people as CEO of RushmoreDrive.com. I'm constantly striving to recognize, reward, and train high-potential people. First of all, I tell my best people explicitly that they show potential and plan appropriate development to groom their skills. Furthermore, I try to make them feel special; that's the key.

When the Charlotte Hornets were playing against LeBron James and the Cleveland Cavaliers, I gave two tickets to see the highly anticipated game to one member of my high-potential staff. I asked him not to disclose to anyone else at the company that I had offered him the tickets because I didn't want the others to feel slighted or excluded. However, I wanted to make this high-potential staff member know that I think highly of him, will go out of my way for him, and want to mentor and encourage him to stay with us and move up.

Some managers say you should treat everyone the same. Obviously, everyone on your staff deserves respect. But it is acceptable to treat high-potential people differently. I don't have enough NBA tickets to go around and circulate through the staff. But I want the future leaders of my team to know they are loved and respected, and that I'm going to take care of them.

The secrets of keeping high-potential individuals on staff and not lose them to an $8,000 or $12,000 pay increase are very simple. Treat people right. Develop them. Build their career. Challenge them. Make them feel special. Let them know where they fit, long term, into the organization. Pay them well.

Becoming an Employee-Centered Organization

You can cut turnover and retain a much higher percentage of your employees (you are always going to lose some of them) by concentrating on four basic steps.

Step 1: Recognize, Recognize, Recognize

It's that simple. More than salary increases, which can only be given every so often and have a way of fading fast, recognizing

employees for their efforts goes a long way to keeping them. Everyone wants to feel special and valued. The larger the organization,
the more the employee can get lost, becoming another cog in the
organization. But when the manager or leader stands up at the
meeting and says, "Mary Difali's efforts helped us gain the new
contract," or, "Sam Smith's hard work helped boost our customer
service numbers," what's the first thing that Mary or Sam says
to their spouse that night? "My manager recognized me for my
efforts. And that made me feel special and valued."

Step 2: Avoid Micromanaging

If there's one thing that most employees despise, it's being micro-
managed. Having a boss look over your shoulder says MISTRUST.
Most people don't want to stay at a job where the boss has no
confidence in them, doesn't trust them, and waits for them to
make a mistake. The opposite of that is trusting your employees
and challenging and supporting them.

Step 3: See Things from the Employee's Viewpoint

Most managers view their employees as a resource. What kind of
work can I get out of them? How can the employee help meet
deadlines? How can I maximize the worth of this employee? All
those questions are valid. But in order to retain your employees,
you need to see matters from their viewpoint.

Think of your employee as your trusted friend. You always want
to support your friends, and yet at times, you must be honest with
them and explain what they've done wrong. It's the same with

your employees. As long as they know you respect them, are on their side, and can provide them with challenging opportunities that stretch their talents, you will retain them.

Help your employees to grow. Assist employees in reaching their long-term goals. Stretch their talents. Update their skills. Invite talented staff members to conferences to expand their network and learn about new trends. Ask yourself, How can I help my employees reach their goals while moving the organization forward? How can I get the most out of my employees and also make sure they get what they want?

Step 4: Specialize in Employee Relations

Just as Nordstrom has dedicated itself to customer service as its signature brand, why can't your organization focus on employee satisfaction as its competitive edge? Imagine how your organization would prosper and change if you heightened retention, kept the best and brightest employees, and curtailed turnover? And imagine the gains if your company became known as the best in your field for treating employees and started attracting the top marketers, financiers, designers, and salespeople. Imagine the ramifications.

Most companies know that keeping an existing customer costs much less than spending valuable marketing dollars finding new customers. Why can't companies spend as much time making their employees happy and focusing on retaining them as they do on recruiting them? And if businesses viewed satisfying employees as they do meeting the needs of customers, retention levels would rise! It is absolutely senseless to spend hundreds of thousands of dollars on recruiting fees, conferences, and recruitment videos and podcasts to find the right people and then ignore them and let many of them walk out the door within the first year.

I recommend organizations spend as much energy and dollars on retaining employees as they do on recruiting them. If organizations spent fifty cents of every dollar on recruiting and the equivalent sum on retaining employees, they'd keep those employees longer. When retention is given the same respect as recruiting, the odds are strong that you will hold on to a much higher percentage of your staff.

Retention Tips from the Chief People Officer at Ticketmaster and Southwest Airlines

Having spent several years as chief people officer at Southwest Airlines and the last year and a half as chief people officer at Ticketmaster, Beverly Carmichael has spent hours thinking about the best ways to retain staff. She employs multiple strategies that are highly effective in an organization's ability to retain employees.

Being Forthright with Employees During the Interview

Too many organizations oversell a job, Carmichael suggests. Many talent acquisition people will say anything to make the job sound appealing to an applicant during the interview to persuade them to take the job. People know and understand that every job has good and not-so-good aspects, and when interviewing, they expect to hear it all. If the applicant begins work and realizes that the actual job fails to live up to the promises, then that disappointment and frustration can easily lead to the new hire leaving within a year. Practice what you preach, Carmichael urges HR and talent staff. "One of the biggest turnoffs that can lead to attrition is making promises that you can't keep and people realizing they weren't given the true picture of the job," she says.

Her advice: Describe the job as honestly and forthrightly as possible. Give job candidates the true picture of how demanding the job is, how often they may have to work late, what the limitations are, as well as the fun aspects and growth opportunities within the position. If you paint a realistic portrait of what the job entails, the odds are stronger that you'll get the best candidate, someone who will last at the job, rather than someone who will be unhappy during the first week and grow unhappier after that. "If you're straight with people, you're more likely to find people who are right for the job and who will thrive in your company and stay. If you find people attracted to what you sold them and it wasn't true, you're going to lose them anyway," Carmichael says.

Identifying the Right Managers

Retaining people revolves around finding managers who know how to treat people. People essentially work for other people, and if they feel valued on the job, they'll stay. If they feel belittled, they'll leave at the first offer. "Organizations need to make sure they have leaders who are influencing other people positively. In my work, the biggest factor that determines who stays and who leaves are the leaders," Carmichael asserts.

Retention Is More Than Just a Numbers Game

Of course, some people will leave. Ironically, Carmichael says, the companies that succeed in retaining their best staff are willing to let poor performers go. The companies that coddle people, protect the weakest performers, and keep people with bad attitudes often have the highest attrition rates, she suggests. The best employees want to work with other good employees and want to be challenged by their colleagues.

Furthermore, Carmichael contends that judging a staff by attrition and retention percentages tells only half the story. Some CEOs demand that the attrition rate be held to a certain percentage. But Carmichael says what really matters is who stays and who leaves, not the numbers. The C performers should improve their performance or leave to find more suitable positions. You want the high performers to stay. Attrition numbers alone don't tell the entire story and can be misleading.

Attracting the Right People Who Will Stay

From her experience at both Southwest Airlines and Ticketmaster, Carmichael also attests to how important attitude and cultural fit are to hiring.

- ☞ *Hire for attitude and train for skills.* Southwest hires for attitude, not skills. As long as it wasn't selecting a pilot or mechanic, people could be trained to handle customer service jobs. Hire people with the right outgoing attitude, people skills, and sense of humor and they can be trained to handle any job. In fact, Carmichael was a Southwest attorney who wanted new challenges, gained valuable skills as an employment lawyer, had the right attitude, and was named vice president of people (head of HR) as her first HR job.

Southwest also employed behavioral-based interviews to pinpoint candidates who best blended into the culture. Recruiting interviews focused on how candidates behaved in certain situations. For example, "Tell us how you used humor to diffuse a conflict," or "How did you problem-solve when your team couldn't agree?" This type of questioning elicits more revealing answers from a potential job candidate than just asking vaguely about someone's experience or opinion.

☞ *Cultural fit is critical in retention.* Ticketmaster's culture has gone through dramatic changes in its thirty-one-year history. By 2008, the organization had evolved into a nimble culture with little bureaucracy and where people who show initiative can take on numerous challenges and not be boxed in. "If people want everything explicitly defined, this isn't the place for them. We don't define everything in black and white; in fact, most everything is gray," Carmichael notes. The workload encourages flexibility. Ticket demand can be high when a major concert is announced, causing people to be very busy one week. And then demand drops off the next week, so people will be less consumed by that event and more consumed by something else. The day-to-day monotony that can set in at some jobs doesn't happen often at Ticketmaster, where employees must stay nimble. "We have people who are exhilarated because they don't know what they're going to be doing next week," she says.

Two major factors attract people to working at Ticketmaster. One is the leadership team. The second is the challenge of the job. Sean Moriarty has been at Ticketmaster for eight years, the last two as its CEO. He is a charismatic leader who is down to earth and has kept a dedicated team of people intact for years. "It's very clear that we have many highly skilled and talented people that could go anywhere. Many get calls from recruiters, but they want to work for Sean," Carmichael says. When a motivating, dynamic leader sets an energetic tone, it helps retain people in your organization.

Companies that don't have dynamic leaders or a fun atmosphere are sometimes relegated to using money as the main lure to attract staff. Openly and candidly, Carmichael acknowledges that "we don't use salary to lure folks." Salaries are competitive, but the open culture, dynamic atmosphere, room for growth, energized colleagues, informal environment, and great leaders attract most people. If you are trying to keep people with money, you'll lose most times because a competitor is often willing to pay more for a highly coveted employee.

To ensure that Ticketmaster's culture focuses on retaining people, it emphasizes leadership. If leaders motivate staff, retention will be high. If leaders are indifferent to their staff's needs, attrition will rise.

Making a Difference Matters

To retain staff, people need to feel "that what they are doing is making a difference. If they feel recognized for their work, have an opportunity to grow, and can see how their role fits into the big picture, they'll likely stay," Carmichael says. Some people will leave if they feel trapped, have limited opportunity, or don't connect with their boss.

Financials as a Retention Tool

Despite the fact that Carmichael has downplayed the role of money to woo staff, she acknowledges that compensation plans and incentives play a role in retaining people. When Carmichael was an HR executive at Southwest Airlines, her contract included a ten-year vesting schedule. That meant she needed to stay at Southwest for ten years to exercise all of her stock options. It was no coincidence that those vesting rights were a strong incentive for her and one reason she spent ten years at the airline. "It's a lot easier to jump ship when you financially have nothing to lose," Carmichael says. Even though recognition, leadership development, and training are critical retention tools, financial incentives can also encourage people to stay.

Getting Staff to Fall in Love with the Company

As this chapter has demonstrated, it takes many methods to retain your best talent, including paying people fairly, treating them right, training them, developing employees with high potential, and doing all of the little things that makes people feel special and valued.

Herb Kelleher mastered the little details, which helped employees at Southwest Airlines fall in love with the company. When he personally signed and sent birthday cards to every Southwest employee, the message delivered was clear: We care about you and we recognize that everyone at Southwest makes a difference, not just the executive team. That's why their retention level was the highest in the airline industry. Having a CEO who is accessible to all the staff, not sequestered in his office and talking only to his direct reports, further forged employee loyalty. By developing a strong rapport with each worker—which can more easily be done when the organization is small—the leader is encouraging employees to fall in love with the company. When an offer from an executive recruiter comes in, the leader wants the employee to say, "I don't want to disappoint my boss who cares about me."

For the companies that want to succeed in a knowledge economy, retention can be their competitive edge. Beverly Carmichael has offered concrete retention tips used at Southwest Airlines and Ticketmaster. Companies such as Goldman Sachs or Google, which are industry leaders, have been successful at retaining people, too. But even they have to worry about the young upstart competition that can offer employees more to do and greater challenges. Retaining employees is thus a continual quest.

Ultimately, what does it take to encourage your employees to fall in love with the company? Knowing staff well. Knowing what motivates each employee. Recognizing employees for their efforts. Rewarding them in the ways that enthuse them. Making sure managers treat them right. Building esprit de corps and camaraderie on the team. Creating an environment of authenticity where people are free to express themselves. All those factors come into play in the quest to retain employees, keeping them as long as you can, knowing that these days most employees expect to be free agents. Keeping your employees for three to five years and retaining your best employees for a longer term can be a realistic goal if you become an employee-centered organization that encourages your employees to fall in love with the company.

CHAPTER FOUR

♦ ♦ ♦

OBJECTIFYING THE JOB SEARCH

If people are your secret ingredient to success, then finding ways to hire the best people provides your competitive edge. How do you hire the right people? How do you improve your hiring strategies to ensure that you are selecting the right people to succeed? How can you create criteria that identify the best person based on a sound, objective approach rather than intuition or conjecture? Devising specific approaches to objectify hiring will heighten your chances of finding talented people who can give your organization a competitive edge.

A November 16, 2008, *Fortune* article, "Great People Decisions: Why They Matter So Much," described a host of CEOs who failed and identified one major reason for their collapse: their inability to identify talented, competent people. More than any other factor, their failures were attributable to their not being able to put the right people in the right jobs. When CEOs appoint the wrong people to senior-level positions, those appointed individuals often (and not surprisingly) make decisions that negatively impact the organization's viability. Making bad people decisions stalls, stymies, and paralyzes business. And yet organizations continue to make the same hiring mistakes. Why?

In my opinion, most organizations go wrong because they make their hiring choices subjectively—hiring based on a subjective *feeling* that this person is right for the job. The hiring or line managers sense intuitively that the applicant fits the job, and often that feeling is based on some initial rapport or connection between the interviewer and the applicant.

Despite what Malcolm Gladwell wrote in *Blink* about the wisdom of first impressions, often this quick and subjective evaluation leads to hiring a person who isn't qualified for the job, doesn't fit into the culture, and lasts a very short time. In some cases, for example, choosing a new employee happens because of the "six degrees of separation" approach. During the interview, it turns out that the interviewer and applicant were alumni of the same university, grew up in the same city, root for the Green Bay Packers, or once attended the same summer camp. That instant connection and familiarity might mean you'd make great after-work drinking buddies, but job success is dependent on prior success, concrete skills, technical knowledge, and communication ability, not whether two people are simpatico or favor the same football team.

If "people" are what serve as the catalyst to energize an organization, then hiring the right people is the glue that determines long-lasting success. And yet most organizations treat hiring the way people judge their hairstyles: If it feels right, go with it. This may work for haircuts but not for hiring in a complex and highly global business environment.

Most times, basing hiring on concrete criteria such as the 360-degree performance standard leads to choosing the best candidate. And yet there is something to be said for listening to one's gut reaction. Even when basing a job search on objective standards, if your gut says that the candidate is too slick, too practiced, or too robotic, then listening to your gut (more about that later in the chapter) can be entered into the hiring equation. Most important, however, is that objective criteria, based on prior success standards, form the basis of the job search.

I recommend three major ways to change the way you hire in your organization that can transform your entire approach to finding new talent:

1. Objectify the job search by developing the best predictors of successful performance on the job.

2. Pinpoint and specify exactly what the job is, what the criteria are for evaluating the job, and the outcomes that must emanate from the job. Too many organizations use only a vague job description or a murky sense of what the job is and the qualities and skills of the person sought for the job. That makes hiring the right person nearly impossible.

3. Ensure that the person fits the company's culture. What works at IBM may not be deemed success at Monsanto.

Defining the Strategy

Since every company must have a clear strategic management approach that will guide its future, defining that approach is necessary before embarking on any job search. If Microsoft's strategy for 2008 and beyond is to extend its influence and revenue on the Internet and move away from designing software in a box, that overall vision will guide its hiring in the next few years. Hence, defining the company's vision for the future, its prescription for revenue growth, leads the hiring process.

Once that overall strategy is determined, then its execution can be broken down into functional strategies, such as human resources, financial, legal, marketing, and information technology strategies.

A 1998 study of 275 portfolio managers by Ernst & Young, "Measures That Matter," cited that the ability to execute strategy transcended the importance of the strategy itself. Experts say that organizations have problems implementing strategies because in a knowledge economy, the intangibles such as customer relationships, innovative products and services, employee skills and motivation, information technology and databases, take precedence over the old-fashioned tangible assets. Robert S. Kaplan and David P. Norton in *The Strategy-Focused Organization* noted that most organizations still implement strategy in a command-and-control way, but businesses are changing so rapidly that organizations need to be more flexible and give individual business and team leaders more autonomy. Their solution involves organizational alignment where teams translate the company's overall strategy specifically into their business. For this approach to work, every individual in the organization must know and understand the strategy and translate it into their specific sphere of influence.

What does this mean for your hiring? Every person involved in the hiring team must know the organization's overarching strategy and use it as a basis for considering the new hire. If Microsoft is moving from a software company to an Internet advertising company, then hiring should take into consideration its new strategy for revenue growth in the future.

Step 1: Objectify the Job Search

Most organizations use vague language and general job descriptions as a basis for hiring the right person. Frankly, you would be better off using a blank piece of paper to guide the candidate selection process. Most job descriptions are written by someone in HR, so they lack specification, don't fully explain the job, avoid outcomes, and ignore the organization's culture. Instead, the first thing to do is to determine what the best predictors of successful performance for this particular job are. If the job entails developing new sales leads and communicating with existing customers to boost sales, then those outcomes must form the basis of the job description. If the job is community outreach, then the applicant's proven ability to connect to neighborhood organizations and other groups may serve as the best indicator. In short, the job descriptions must really describe the job.

Determining the best predictors of a job requires due diligence and research. HR and the line managers should, for example, go directly to the last person or people who performed the job and ask them outright, "What exactly did you do?" What were the key functions you needed to perform? What determined your effectiveness? What did our customers want from you? What were the outcomes required of the job? How did you add value? How did you contribute to the company's return on investment (ROI)?

When working on a job spec (as HR people call it), one trap to avoid is writing a boilerplate description. *Be specific.* Don't just write "performs market research" (which is vague and nebulous), but specifically use words that describe what it means (i.e., "conducts nationwide qualitative research using focus groups"). Using specific language, the HR and line managers can see exactly what the job is and then elicit from the applicant whether the candidate has performed that task in the past. During an interview, the HR person can ask the candidate to describe the last nationwide qualitative research she performed. How did she launch the project? What determined its success? What obstacles did she face, and how were they overcome?

Rather than just relying on hiring managers to write job descriptions, I recommend taking more of a 360-degree approach to developing a job description. In 360-degree performance management, you get feedback from managers, supervisors, peers, and customers; likewise, the 360-degree job description approach is based on input and feedback from a variety of stakeholders: people who have done the job in the past, the manager who supervises the person on the job, colleagues who team with the person, customers, and HR. Combine all of their comments, feedback, and elements and you can objectify what you are seeking from the new hire.

Getting feedback from people who have been in the job in the last few years is crucial. They know what works, what doesn't work, and the skills required to do the job well. Ask them to describe the qualities, skills, and temperament of the ideal person for the job. Colleagues who collaborate with the person can offer insight into the tasks done, the problems that need to be solved, and the signs that determine customer success. Managers can offer an entirely other view. Does the person exceed expectations? Does the staff support colleagues? Is the person providing superior customer service? Customer feedback can be formidable since customers ultimately determine an organization's success. Finally, HR can see where the person fits into the entire organization and how the employee is doing compared to colleagues. Put all of these elements together, and that job description is going to be written in a specific, thorough, and comprehensive way.

If done well, the 360-degree job description covers technical skills, qualities and personality traits, outcomes, and actions expected. This detailed job description results in a thorough analysis of what the ideal candidate will need to do on the job. It can reveal, for example, that hiring an accountant who is competent in technical skills but can't communicate with clients may be the wrong choice if the accountant must influence clients and make recommendations to ensure that organization's policies are followed.

The more objective 360-degree job description should also include the "intangibles," the areas that most traditional job descriptions miss. For example, does the successful candidate for a particular job need strong consensus-building skills because the team makes joint decisions? Or must the applicant be a self-starter because the manager is based in Denver and most of the team members are scattered around the country and communicate virtually? Does the boss demand that the team stay until 6 p.m.? In hiring, personality traits play as important a role as technical skills. In customer service, the ability to be patient, possess thick skin, and be resilient are as crucial to success as computer skills. If you are an audit manager, the ability to communicate with financial people who are ruled by numbers is just as important as knowing accounting standards. All of these details, when included in a job description, can make the difference between hiring failure and success.

There is one other very important reason organizations should work to objectify the job search process—and that's litigation avoidance. In these days of class-action employment-related lawsuits, organizations cannot afford to have a questionable job search process. If the person ultimately selected for a role does not possess all of the required skills and qualities, you or the company could face legal issues. For example, in a previous business at which I worked, we were seeking a person with ten-plus years of senior-level management experience. We asked an executive recruiter to fill the job, and he supplied about fifty resumes of people with this requisite experience. We whittled the list to five people and started interviewing them. But then one person on the search committee said she knew someone who would be perfect for the role, although the candidate only had five years of experience. We liked his resume, brought him in, interviewed him, and preferred him to the other candidates who had more experience. When we decided to make the offer to this candidate, who did not meet many of the "requirements" we detailed in our own job description, another unsuccessful candidate filed an EEOC suit, claiming, among other things, that the whole interview process was a sham and part of a pattern and practice of illegal discrimination in violation of the Civil Rights Act. We spent literally hundreds of thousands of dollars defending a claim that was totally avoidable had we been true to our own hiring process by interviewing only candidates that met the qualifications we outlined in the job description.

The 360-degree job description guides you to hiring the right person and reduces the chances of falling prey to six degrees of separation or choosing someone because it feels right, which almost always leads to disaster. Without the fully developed job description, a hiring manager is like an archer trying to hit the bull's-eye blindfolded.

There are two morals here: (1) Hire the wrong person and the person will fail, leading to more turnover, reduced morale, time wasted on finding a replacement, and more wasted money; and (2) if you create a thorough job description and fail to hire someone who lives up to the description, your organization can be sued.

Step 2: Create a Strategy for Talent Acquisition

After you've done a thorough job of writing the 360-degree job description, you need to create a strategy for finding the right person. That's where your talent acquisition specialist can play a major role. Should you post the job on major online Internet job sites that attract thousands of job seekers, or TheLadders.com for six-figure jobs, or RushmoreDrive.com for diverse candidates? Or should you use niche job sites? Or do you go to a specialized executive recruiter if you recognize the job will be hard to fill? If you are a small business owner and strapped for time, how can you conduct the search as expeditiously as possible without short-changing it?

To select the best vehicle for finding talent, you'll need to answer a host of questions. Let's say you are you looking for an accountant in Chicago. Is relocation included? If not, are you looking in Chicago and the suburbs? The last person had six years' experience when starting, so is that the required background or could a more junior person handle the job?

If I'm looking for an experienced accountant and paying $60,000, is that the going rate? Am I offering enough money, and do I need to pay a bonus? Identifying how to find the right candidate is equivalent to launching a marketing campaign. How do I target the right candidate? How do I narrow down my search? Which vehicles—for example, niche websites or your own contacts—will produce the candidates who possess the right background and attributes? That's a host of consequential questions that must be answered after the 360-degree job description has been completed.

Step 3: Sifting Through Resumes

If you place a job advertisement on the large job-searching websites, you are likely to receive hundreds if not thousands of resumes. The HR function is tasked with narrowing down those stacks of resumes into five or ten candidates, depending on the job.

What guides the streamlining process is the 360-degree job description. Once you determined the specifics of what you are looking for in terms of experience, skills, temperament, and training, you can begin to eliminate many resumes that don't match the job. Here are some tips:

- Frequently, many people eliminate themselves. The waitress who applies for a marketing director's role is clearly out of her league. The people who have misspellings and grammatical errors on their resume have eliminated themselves as well.

☞ Look for two other signs to rule out people. A person who has had eight jobs in ten years moves around too much and is too risky to be considered. On the other hand, someone who has been at one job for eighteen years is likely to have problems adapting to change, and at most dynamic companies, change is the name of the game.

☞ Look for industry-specific background. If a money-center bank is seeking a financial planner, the odds are that it will seek someone with experience in financial services. However, sometimes a bank might want a fresh approach and could easily hire someone from a related industry, such as an insurance company, where the adjustment will be minor. On the other hand, if a hospital is seeking a specialist in Medicaid reimbursement, it won't hire someone with experience at an Internet entertainment company.

☞ Remember also that resumes don't tell a person's full job history. These days everyone has multiple resumes. So the financial planner is also a financial counselor, a money manager, a claims adjustor, and a sales manager. Anyone can manipulate or arrange a resume to suit many jobs. Some people withhold dates from their resume, too. Often they don't want to reveal that they graduated from college in 1970 because that means they are fifty years plus. It's perfectly acceptable, though, for an HR employee to ask an applicant to fill in dates of service or experience; there's nothing illegal about that.

Hence, employees are forbidden to ask birth dates but can elicit work-related experience and dates.

Step 4: Employing Behavioral Interviewing

Before people knew about behavioral interviewing, the interviewing process involved asking softball questions such as, "Tell me about your last job. What are your key strengths? What are your career aspirations?" These questions were intended to keep the applicant at ease and to yield a slight sense of the person, but frankly never scratched the surface or gave any in-depth indication of whether the applicant could handle the job.

What's mission critical here is filling that job description, doing the job right, and helping the company meet its goals. Identifying the right person involves zeroing in on the skills and personality required to do the task; it's not a popularity contest or dating show. One of the best ways to achieve the goal of objectifying the job search is to employ behavioral interviewing.

Industrial psychologists developed behavioral interviewing in the 1970s based on the theory that past performance is the most powerful indicator of future success. Rather than asking vague and nebulous questions such as "Tell me about yourself, your strengths and weaknesses," behavioral interviewing discovers what the candidate has done and accomplished on the job and how he went about achieving those outcomes.

Questions should be worded in a way to elicit anecdotes and performance information. You might break down your questions into subjects such as decision making, leadership, innovation, and motivation. On decision making, you could ask: Can you cite an example of when you had to make an immediate decision based on having insufficient information? What were the results? What did you learn? On leadership, questions can be: What was the most difficult group you ever had to lead? Cite examples of people who thwarted getting the job done. What specifically did you do to integrate them into the group and enable them to work with the group? On motivation, a question might be: How do you feel you've gone beyond your job description? On innovation: What was the most innovative idea you ever suggested? What was the outcome of it? By using the 360-degree job description, you can develop specific, pointed questions that will elicit details on the applicant's past performance and help you objectify your job search.

If you are following my lead and have the detailed job description written and ready, it will serve as a guideline. If the description says the job entails handling a new Internet marketing campaign, you can elicit from the applicant recent brands that she has represented and what specific campaigns she helped lead. How did you come up with the idea? How was the campaign structured? What media was used to promote it? What was the major obstacle on the campaign? How did you overcome it? What problems developed between the client and the marketing approach that you had to overcome? How was it solved? What metrics were used to measure the campaign's success? What about the campaign was different? Was it eye-catching, iconoclastic, or out-of-the-box? Those answers will fit the job description.

Besides skills, you are looking to determine the candidate's character. Sometimes just having skills isn't enough to succeed. You need to possess the intangibles: persistence and resiliency. To assess how resilient the person is, you might ask: What went wrong on the campaign? How were problems overcome? What would you do differently? What was the key thing you learned?

If your culture revolves around team building, questions can be constructed to elicit whether the person is a team player or a lone wolf. Can you cite examples of how you worked with others? How do you bring out the best in people, and how do colleagues bring out the best in you? Were there difficult people you had to work with, and how were you able to collaborate with them despite the differences? Questions should focus on the person's temperament and personality and how that fits into your organization's culture.

Once you blend in the applicant's experience and skills, problem-solving ability, and personality, you should have a good picture of whether someone is right for the job, and it is an objective assessment, regardless of whether you and the applicant went to the same college, play golf at the same club, or attended the same summer camp.

Avoiding the Traps

There are many pitfalls to be aware of during the interview process. They range from making decisions based on likeability to the tendency to create unrealistic deadlines or to be too inflexible. Here are the major traps to avoid.

Trap 1: The Likeability Trap

Many interviewers think that if they like or feel comfortable with the person they are interviewing, share a similar sense of humor, wear similar khaki pants and blue button-down shirts, then the person fits the organization. If the person is deficient in certain skills, the interviewer reasons, it can be learned on the job. But if you need an experienced project manager for a major construction site, or a software engineer, or a manager for a nonprofit, whether or not you like the person cannot drive the decision. What matters most is whether the person has performed similar work or faced similar challenges in the past. Does the person have the right skills? And will the individual's personality fit the culture? Does the applicant add value to the company?

Instant rapport sometimes happens. The interviewer and the applicant hit it off, but identifying the best candidate for the job is not the same as choosing a person to have beers with after work. Getting along on the job plays a role, but it is secondary to whether the person has the right skills, temperament, and experience to do the job well over the long haul.

Trap 2: Falling for Attractive People

Too many hiring managers fall victim to judging people by their looks and demeanor rather than skills. Too many hiring managers I've met assume that most tall men are confident, short men lack confidence, attractive women are appealing, and overweight people are insecure. Another trap in hiring is to immediately fall for people who show presence based on their physical attributes. Though you may be bowled over by someone's good looks or confident demeanor, it does not necessarily mean that candidate possesses the skills to do the job, will live up to your 360-degree job description, and is really the best person to fill the vacancy. You would think that most hiring managers would overcome their stereotypes or expectations based on tall or short men, attractive and svelte or overweight women, but many have not.

If you are interviewing for a pharmaceutical sales representative, the attractiveness of the candidate could easily sway you. Since the sales rep has to build rapport quickly and make a strong impression, the applicant's looks could play a superficial role in job success. But the trap is hiring an attractive sales rep who lacks the intelligence to sell the product and lacks the communication skills necessary to present cogent information about the product's strengths. Looks aren't everything. If the person isn't articulate and doesn't represent the company well, then the attractive woman or tall guy is a liability, not an asset.

I once interviewed a woman for a job who walked into the room and was so overwhelmingly gorgeous that I had to work really hard to focus on the real purpose of our meeting—to find the most qualified candidate. I reminded myself that I needed to hire someone who lived up to the 360-degree job description, fit into the culture, and would stay with the company for several years to create stability. I focused on the objective criteria we used to hire someone, rather than being swayed by her attractiveness.

We're human. Sometimes we become mesmerized by people's looks and want to hire them because they are so physically attractive. That's the trap. The focus should be on whether the applicant, attractive or not, can do the job as determined by the well-thought-out and detailed job description.

Hence, you need to know your own biases and transcend them. If attractive people influence your thoughts and you unconsciously think they'll do a better job, overcome that impulse by returning to the job description. The focus of hiring someone must be on skills, experience, communication ability, and fit with the corporate culture, not a person's sexiness or attractiveness. If you demean overweight people and stereotype them, first make yourself aware of that fact and then use that trusty job description as a guide to rule the job search. This isn't a beauty pageant.

Stereotypes of good-looking people can also undermine them. If you think most attractive blondes are ditzy, start reevaluating that fallacy. If you think overweight men are sloppy or incompetent, you are prejudging them and treating them unfairly. Knowing your biases is the first step to overcoming them and judging people on their own merits, based on the job description, regardless of pigmentation, ethnicity, or looks.

Trap 3: Avoiding the Ism Traps—Racism, Sexism, Homophobia, and Other Prejudgments

As a former general counsel, I must also stress that certain questions should be avoided based on legal grounds. For example, you shouldn't be asking whether someone is married, has children, or is pregnant, or what church they belong to or whom they voted for in the last election.

When hiring managers make assumptions about disabled people, pregnant women (or any woman), African Americans, Latinos, Native Americans, Jehovah's Witnesses, Muslims, or any other group of people, problems arise. These problems are legal ones, because people cannot be prevented from competing for a job due to their race, natural origin, religion, or gender, as well as pragmatic, because you may lose the best people to your competitor. Moreover, since most markets are global, organizations need a diverse, multicultural staff that understands their wide-ranging customers. Shutting people out because they look different, have an accent, or use a wheelchair is unacceptable and bad business.

If you rely on the 360-degree job description to provide your hiring compass, you will be led in the right direction. If the job requires traveling to customer sites 100 days out of the year and the woman you are interviewing brings up the fact that she refuses to travel because she wants to be home with her children after school, she doesn't meet the job's qualifications. She can be disqualified. But if the woman is pregnant and you assume that she won't stay in the job long because she'll likely leave to raise her child, you are treating her unfairly and prejudging her.

Companies spend considerable dollars on diversity training, and these workshops can directly affect and improve a company's hiring policy. Learning to treat each person fairly and overcoming preconceived notions about a person's gender, race, and background can lead to hiring the best people who fit the job and possess the right qualifications.

Trap 4: Rushing the Job Selection

The Paul Simon lyric, "Slow down, you move too fast," might serve as perfect advice for many job searches. At most companies, however, the pace of many job searches is desperate, frantic, and urgent. A project manager resigns and has found a better job. If a new project manager isn't found within three weeks, deadlines may not be met and the company may be fined thousands of dollars for lateness. The stakes are high, and the tendency is to create an unrealistic deadline and force hiring someone by the end of the week. "We have got to find a body to replace the project manager" is the prevailing tone. That's a no-no.

Rushing a job search is equivalent to forcing something to happen without stopping to think and without first creating a well-thought-out strategy and conducting your due diligence. My advice: Give yourself time. Take two weeks and find the right person, rather than conducting a frantic, rushed, desperate search. More often than not, those "overnight" job searches result in finding someone who can't do the job, which necessitates repeating the entire process all over again. Instead, take two weeks, do it right, find the right person, and keep that person in place for several years to come.

Trap 5: Having Too Many Cooks Spoils the Meal

When the James Beard Foundation, one of the country's leading culinary associations, bestows its award for best chef of the year, the statuette goes to one chef, not ten sous-chefs who helped prepare the meal. That's because one chef must be in charge. Many companies have moved toward consensus building, which often allows teams of several people, sometimes even a dozen staffers, to conduct interviews of an applicant to make sure the person gets along with the entire team. Letting teams offer feedback can be a very constructive activity, as long as only one or two people are ultimately responsible for making the hiring decision.

If a team member has a certain issue with the candidate, that concern should be raised before the group and vetted. When so many people are involved, overly subjective reactions can adulterate the hiring decision. One staff member says, "I didn't like it when the candidate referred negatively to his last employer." Another team member says, "I thought she carried an attitude," but offers little proof. These highly subjective comments have little or nothing to do with the candidate's experience, skills, or ability to do the job. Most of these comments should be glossed over and ignored. As long as the 360-degree job description is guiding the hiring process and the interviewers are focused on the person's skill and ability to do the job, everything should work out. Just as one chef rules the kitchen, you need one or two people to be in charge of the hiring or the process can go awry.

Trap 6: Uncovering Emotional Intelligence

Interviewing a candidate for forty-five minutes to an hour, reviewing the person's resume and contacting references, asking behavioral questions, and having a team interact with an applicant can reveal many facets of a person. But the truth is, you can't get to know someone thoroughly in such a short time period. You can only make an educated guess about the candidate's emotional intelligence and competencies.

Some companies use Myers-Briggs and other psychological assessments to add to the entire picture of a person and help determine if the person fits into the organization's culture. I see these tests as one more data point or tool to consider in the entire evaluation.

Having a team interview a person provides feedback from many vantage points. While most people who conduct the interviewing aren't trained psychologists, the advantage of having multiple interviewers is that they'll ask diverse behavioral questions that can help detect if someone is defensive and feels angry or threatened when questioned. Group interviews can uncover some of a person's emotional intelligence. The key here is asking open-ended questions that will reveal a person's personality and ability to handle conflict, deal with pressures and deadlines, or cope with difficult people on the job.

Trap 7: Relying Too Much on the Internet

Think of how easy the Internet makes the job search. You sit at your desk, write a job description, post it on the Internet job boards and voila, hundreds of resumes are delivered to your e-mail box. You didn't have to leave your cubicle because the resumes and e-mails are sent electronically. But sorting through hundreds of resumes can take a day or more of your time if you conduct thorough due diligence. And many of these resumes are a waste of your time because they are far off-target and are sent by supermarket cashiers who dream about becoming chief information officers.

If you are using the major Internet hiring sites, you need to create a template of exactly what you are looking for and how you are going to screen the resumes, because you don't want to spend two weeks of your time collecting and analyzing hundreds of resumes. Beyond the job description, you need to look for key phrases to ensure the applicant fits the job and you are not being misled.

The Internet can also serve as a great tool to conduct research for a job search. Using Goggle or Ask.com, you can find job descriptions at Bank of America or Citigroup, for example, if you are seeking to find an accountant or auditor.

Even the social networking sites can play a revealing role in a job search, particularly if you are interviewing Generation X or Y applicants who are more prone to use these sites. A description on Facebook or MySpace can uncover whether the person is prone to behavior that may not fit into your culture or, conversely, has some hidden talent that may fit in and add value.

Trap 8: Not Making Adjustments to the Hiring Process When It's Clear You Didn't Get It Right

I'm reminded of one of the most difficult searches I've ever conducted. The CEO tapped me to find him an executive assistant. I followed all of the "right" steps to conduct the search. I interviewed the CEO to understand exactly what he wanted in an EA, and then I spoke with the person who had recently left the role. The one thing I knew was that executive assistants to a CEO play such an important role and are so highly valued that many earn six-figure salaries and possess graduate degrees. As such, this assignment was going to be a much more complex job than one might assume.

We posted the job, reviewed a hundred resumes, winnowed them down to ten, and shared them with the CEO. The CEO scrutinized every resume and rejected every single one. All the CEO would say is, "None of these candidates fit what I'm looking for." I explained that each candidate was well qualified and possessed all of the requisite experience, but he still wasn't satisfied. Finally, after beating my head against the wall, I arranged another meeting with the CEO to better understand what I was not delivering and learned that he and I did not get the first step right—the job description. What became very clear is that he wanted an office manager, executive assistant, and a personal assistant—all rolled into one person. My CEO wanted an executive assistant like the one played by Anne Hathaway in *The Devil Wears Prada*—someone who picks up the boss's (in the movie, Meryl Streep's) laundry from the dry cleaner and buys a steak for her lunch, maintains her calendar, takes calls from senior executives, and trains new staff to ensure the office runs properly.

Hence, we had to start our search all over again and update the job description to look for an executive secretary plus a personal assistant plus an office manager. This time, I went to great lengths to draft a new job description that detailed the three primary aspects of the job, which included spending 70 percent of the time as office manager, 20 percent as executive assistant, and 10 percent as personal assistant. I also posted the position on a different set of niche websites that would enhance the chances of finding the types of people who would have these experiences. The lesson is simple: You need to remain willing to change your course of action if it's clear your plan is not producing the right results.

Trap 9: Ignoring Your Gut Instincts

In this chapter, I've emphasized hiring someone based on objective criteria, where skills, experience, personality, and fit with the culture dictate whether the person is the best candidate. Having said that, you still need to rely on your gut instincts.

For example, I once interviewed a woman for a top-level management job. When I asked how much she made at her last job, she said $180,000. I know the pay scale at most companies and knew she was exaggerating. I called her on it, and she hemmed, hawed, and fudged her response. It was clear that she was lying, but she never took responsibility for exaggerating her salary. During the interview, some of her comments were acerbic, but she had all the qualifications and the right experience and solid recommendations, and I hired her despite my reservations. After two weeks on the job, my concerns were playing out in the workplace; she didn't get along with other colleagues and she had a habit of "fudging" answers so we dismissed her. In this case, even though she had the right experience and met many of the job's criteria, she failed in personality, temperament, ethics, and ability to fit into a consensus culture. Had I followed my gut instincts, I would have hired someone else. The moral here is that the job description guides you along the hiring process, but your gut instincts still play a role.

Collaborating with Executive Recruiters

Many people have misconceptions about using executive recruiters. The perception is that companies only use them for a high-level job search for a CEO or CFO. Strapped for time and with HR departments that are overwhelmed, many companies employ executive recruiters on retainer to perform ongoing job searches for a host of jobs, ranging from executive assistants to call center staff and salespeople, not just CEOs. Smaller companies that have two human resources people often rely heavily on search firms.

The emphasis on using the 360-degree job description and focusing on objectifying the search remains even if you use executive recruiters. In that situation, you must describe in detail what you are looking for and provide all of the background material and job descriptions to the outside search firm, to ensure that the search emphasizes the criteria that you have decided on.

One Other Major Factor to Consider in the Objective Job Search

As I detailed in chapter 3, hiring for an extended period of three to five years is the goal. If you sense that the person is overly ambitious and is likely to use the job as a steppingstone and exit after a year, you might be better off choosing an equally qualified person who is more likely to stay a longer period.

One way to heighten your chances of finding a person for the long haul, as Beverly Carmichael from Ticketmaster noted in the last chapter, is to be as honest, forthright, and as detailed as possible about what the job entails. Too many employers hide details that they expect the applicant doesn't want to hear. Staying late, dealing with difficult clients, and traveling 25 percent of the time are the kinds of details that might be withheld. Then the new hire finds out the real deal, feels misled and deceived, and decides to seek a new job within six months of starting. You will be better served if you lay out all of the specifics of the job, because then you'll be able to create a better fit between the new hire and the job, which will lead you to the right person.

Ascertaining how a job candidate responds to change is also important. Nearly every job goes through change on an annual basis. Auto mechanics have to learn computing; product designers have to master computer-assisted design software. Be sure to ask questions of all your job candidates to ascertain how they adapt to change. If you learn that they are good at making adjustments, they may stay longer on the job.

Tips from a Talent Acquisition Director

Don W. Troupe, Jr., is chief talent officer at the Mortgage Broadcast Network, which launched in early 2008 as a Los Angeles–based website and cable network that provides news and information to the global real estate and finance industries. Despite the woes over foreclosures and mortgage defaults, bankers and financial insiders needed guidance on fluctuating mortgage rates and changes in the industry so ironically it was a good time to launch a mortgage network. Over the last fifteen years, he has served in human resources roles at Fortune 500 companies such as IAC/InterActive Corp., Yahoo, and Disney.

Creating Alignment

To ensure the organization is hiring the best person for the job, there must be alignment between the hiring teams and HR. Troupe describes this alignment as making sure that both HR and hiring managers are on the same page about major projects that will be worked on and deliverables that must be completed, and describing the personality type that best fits the team. Most job descriptions include bullet points of the skills and experience required for the job, but he recommends going beyond them to encompass the project's overall goals. "That enables the applicant to conceptualize growth opportunities, know which client groups the candidate will be interfacing with, and better grasp what the job will entail," he says. This more descriptive outlook gives the candidate a fuller view of where he fits in to the organization, what the group demands, and whether he will grow in the job in the next few years, which can heighten the chances of choosing the right person and increasing retention.

For example, when Troupe was at Yahoo and hiring a candidate to redesign the company's search technology, which was a stealth project and not publicized, the job description included details on the product's contribution to current/future revenue streams, the specific projects that would be worked on, the groups that the hire would collaborate with, and the skills and experience required. A job description that includes the fuller department or business unit overview informs the candidate of how and where he'll blend into the team and the organization.

Often, when it came to filling very skilled high-tech jobs at IAC and Yahoo, Troupe's experience was that the demand outstripped the supply. Therefore, the job description not only served as a way to describe the position and select the right person, but it was *the best way* to attract and entice candidates, both "active" and "passive," in the employment market. In fact, according to

Troupe, "That job description may be the only opportunity you're going to get to attract the candidate" given the myriad of opportunities being advertised.

Companies like Yahoo and IAC are seeking A-list candidates who most likely already have a job and aren't actively looking for a new opportunity. Candidates who use major hiring websites enter keyword searches that automatically send descriptions of upcoming jobs that fit their criteria. For example, if Yahoo needed an HTML or Java developer and the job description said the developer would interact with senior management and have an opportunity for lots of creative freedom, it could encourage "passive" candidates to pursue the opportunity. "It could incentivize them to get excited if the position sounded especially appealing," Troupe notes. Hence, the dynamically written job description could motivate the satisfied jobholder to seek a new challenge or to pursue a job that might be a steppingstone in someone's career.

Notice that Troupe didn't mention salary as a way to lure applicants. Most times what entices people to seek a new position is the challenge of the job. How it stretches their talents and fits into their long-term growth objectives can be more important than making thousands of dollars. "The purpose is to get someone motivated about the job from a longevity standpoint and where the job could take their career," he notes. If the motivation is strong, the salary can often be negotiated.

Preplanning the Interview

Asked what tips he could offer on interviewing an applicant, Troupe said he prefers to emphasize preparations that need to take place before the interview happens. Since most times teams are interviewing a prospective candidate, Troupe wants to make sure everyone involved in the job search is on the same page. Everyone must know not only what's in the job description, but also the core attributes that the position demands, what specific role the person will play, the teams the person will interact with, and what specific qualities are the best match for the position. He would meet with teams to prepare a "game plan," just as a football coach readies a team on game day.

HR should provide hiring managers and their interview teams with specific training on how to conduct competency-based interviewing (CBI) or behavioral-interviewing techniques (BIT). CBI focuses on core strengths, character, and aptitude, whereas BIT zeroes in on attitude, approach, and responsiveness. The goal is to make sure HR and business partners are aligned on which criteria they will use to evaluate the candidate's skills, experience, and cultural fit. To eliminate redundancies and save time, each interviewer is assigned a task to elicit comments on skills, experience, or cultural fit. In addition, staff should be trained to examine the candidate's critical thinking, core strengths, intellect, and aptitude. These are the complex skills that don't emerge from someone's resume.

For example, when Troupe was at IAC, he was involved in a job search for a product manager that was joining an established team. Most members had been with the team for eight to ten years and were very experienced, disciplined, and logical thinkers. In addition, this group operated like a family, had weekly outings after work, and sought someone who could fit in both socially and technically. To address these issues, Troupe and the hiring managers collaborated on competency-based and behavioral-interviewing techniques to determine which candidates fit the job and the group. Was the candidate a logical thinker? Did the candidate engage with work and teammates or prefer working alone? If questions are framed appropriately in the competency-based approach, HR and the hiring manager should get a pretty clear picture of whether the applicant is right for the job and will blend in with the group.

Hiring for the Long Haul

No one can ever really discern whether a candidate will prosper in the job and last ten years or flounder and look for another position within a year. To gauge whether someone is right for the job and likely to last for several years, Troupe focuses on determining whether the applicant's core values coalesce with the organization's values.

IAC, for example, stressed customer excellence and integrity, among other qualities, as its core values. Using competency-based questions, Troupe would elicit whether the candidate possessed customer service skills and displayed honesty as a main attribute. If your boss asked you to do something unethical, how would you handle it? If a customer had a complaint but was screaming at you, what would you do? If the candidate's attributes revealed a strong moral character and a dedication to customer satisfaction, Troupe concluded the person was likely to last at IAC.

Anticipating Your Hiring Needs (Don't Just Sit Back)

Some organizations recruit only when a vacancy arises, an approach that's fraught with difficulty and often leads to rushed and last-minute hiring. But the organizations that display best practices opt for a talent acquisition strategy that is always seeking new employees in *anticipation* of vacancies arising. Recruiting may serve as the engine of a hiring strategy, but with a talent acquisition approach, the organization is always building a pipeline of individuals who possess the right skills, Troupe suggests. That pipeline is fed by employee referrals (since employees know the culture better than anyone), by constantly searching for talent on online job websites, and by scouting out the competition. In other words, a myriad of approaches should be used.

Moreover, managers are trained to look for "red flags" among current employees who may be seeking other positions or may be losing their motivation. When employees disengage, show a lack of enthusiasm, are out sick for many days, arrive late, or seem disinterested, they could be signaling that they are looking for other opportunities or souring on their current job or team. Managers are trained to confront the situation and try to engage the employee to feel motivated again, before the employee is lost for good.

Troupe says developing an anticipatory hiring strategy is akin to a company emphasizing its financial growth in the next few quarters. Industry analysts don't just focus on a company's earnings but stress their projected revenue for the next quarter or two. Similarly, talent acquisition leaders can't sit back and say we have everybody in place today; they have to constantly project into the future. What if several of our software developers left this quarter? Or what if several people exited the call center or financial staff? Do we have enough bench strength to replace them? Do we know the talented A-list players at competitors who can be lured to join our team? Are we attending conferences to seek out future

graduates at leading business schools? "Anticipating hiring [needs]
enables a company to operate more strategically, rather than in a
reactionary way," Troupe says.

Seeking Character

In *Emotional Intelligence*, Daniel Goleman discusses how a person's
self-reliance, self-confidence, and resiliency are as important to success as skill-sets. But discerning someone's emotional intelligence
during a couple of forty-five-minute interviews can be a very tricky
proposition. How does Troupe, an experienced talent acquisition
leader, determine whether someone has emotional intelligence,
based on the confines of a job interview? "I evaluate character over
charm," he states. People can be charming, affable, and effervescent,
but those qualities are superficial and will fade. He uses competency-
based interviewing to determine someone's character.

By focusing on an organization's core values, such as integrity,
customer engagement, and consensus building, Troupe can devise
questions that will elicit a person's character. Then he can hone
in on those attributes and begin to evaluate a candidate's character as much as their skills and experience. Since team members
who interview a candidate are focusing on different attributes,
what emerges is a more three-dimensional view of the applicant.
Adding the person's character to experience and skills provides a
fuller view of whether that person is right for the job.

Watching for Traps in the Candidate Search

1. *Contradictions*. Often there's a disparity between what
the candidate includes on the resume and what is

revealed during the interview. For example, the resume may say that Don Smith was responsible for bringing in $2 million of new customers to his old company. During the interview, Smith divulges that it was a team of four people who initiated the $2 million worth of new business. Troupe's reaction is always to vet and investigate the situation more deeply before reaching a conclusion. Did Smith lead the team? Was Smith responsible for 75 percent of the new business? Did Smith lie or just slightly exaggerate? What does this say about his integrity? Can we trust him, or is he prone to being unreliable?

2. *Latecomers.* If Troupe conducts two interviews with a candidate and both times the person is fifteen to thirty minutes late, he begins to wonder about the person's punctuality and character. If the person blames traffic jams in Los Angeles (which are an everyday occurrence) or subway breakdowns in New York (ditto), then the person either doesn't care about being punctual, demonstrates a lack of professionalism, or isn't interested in making a good impression on the interview team. If the person can't get to the interview on time, isn't the applicant likely to be late to work on a recurring basis? Since time is money at most organizations, lateness is unacceptable, unless there is a valid explanation.

3. *Inappropriate Attire or Behavior.* In certain high-tech environments, casual attire is the norm, but there is an unwritten and established dress code as to what is appropriate to wear to job interviews. If the candidate arrives for the interview in flip-flops and shorts, it may indicate that he is not serious about the job, doesn't want to play by the rules, or doesn't really want the job. A certain level of professionalism is expected during the job interview, even if casual attire predominates in certain work environments.

CHAPTER FIVE

♦ ♦ ♦

TRAINING AND DEVELOPMENT: USING T&D TO RETAIN STAFF AND EXECUTE YOUR BUSINESS STRATEGY

In a 2006 study, the Alliance for Excellent Education determined that the nation's colleges and businesses lost $3.7 billion annually due to the massive number of unprepared high school graduates in the workforce. In fact, 42 percent of community college freshmen must enroll in at least one remedial course. Furthermore, in a 2005 study of nearly 1,500 public high school graduates, the nonprofit group Achieve Inc. found that 39 percent—nearly two in five—of recent graduates said there were gaps in their education and they were unprepared to handle basic tasks at work. College instructors found that nearly half of all recent high school graduates were inadequately prepared for college-level math and college-level writing. What do these reports mean for employers? Like it or not, employers must provide basic skills training to their employees.

Employers of all types—for-profit, government, and small business owners—must step in and provide these unprepared high school graduates with basic reading and math skills or suffer the disastrous consequences. Because of this sad commentary on the state of American education, most staff must be trained to master basic reading, writing, and arithmetic, or else business will pay a hefty price.

Imagine if your staff isn't fully literate or can't make change properly or fill out a basic order. What happens when the entry-level person in accounts payable must send out checks if that employee can't compute or read? The potential damage to your company is staggering when checks are distributed with the wrong sum or an extra zero. Imagine how the Target or Wal-Mart cashiers can adversely affect their company if they don't know how to make the right change? Or the effect on customer retention when your call center employees can't write a literate follow-up note to a customer? To ensure that companies are meeting customer needs, basic training must be offered in basic skills, and employees must be tested to prove they have mastered these skills. Making sure employees are literate and possess basic math skills is a prerequisite for any company to succeed.

And it's not just the entry-level employees. Some organizations naively think that if they train their entry-level staff in basic skills that they have fixed the problem. Not necessarily. Supervisors and mid-level managers who communicate with customers, compose written performance appraisals, evaluate employees, and interact with senior managers must also master basic skills. To ensure that no major mishap occurs, employers are increasingly testing staff members on basic skills and then providing organized training to shore up these basic skills. After all, the mid-level manager in an industrial environment who can't read proper directions can cause a major construction incident. In the Internet age, when company gaffes appear online in nanoseconds of any embarrassing incident, an illiterate or poorly worded note from a supervisor can spread like wildfire, causing an organization considerable embarrassment.

Odds are that many members of your staff may change jobs in three to five years. So you might ask, why devote so much time and energy to training if people are going to leave and go to the next shop within a few years? I remember a CEO of a large retailer saying to me: "Why am I going to train someone to go work for my competitor?" I looked him square in the eye and said, "Because you have to, or you won't be in business to have a competitor." My point was simple: If you fail to train your employees for fear they'll simply take your training across the street, your customers will suffer and the competitor across the street will eat your lunch and dinner.

So, training and development are about *survival*. You want to train your people and improve their skills while they are on board because your business success depends on their updating their skills. Status quo in business these days often results in failure. Enhancing their skills makes you more competitive and builds a better workforce for your future, no matter how long staff stays on the job. Furthermore, if your employees see that you are willing to invest in their future, they are likely to remain with you longer (increased retention) and be more productive (increased efficiency and profit).

This chapter explores how "training" differs from "development," and why training is necessary, despite the fact that many employees will move on after three to five years. The chapter will answer these questions: How does training connect into a company's business strategy? What role does training play in retaining talented staff? What determines the right training for each staff member? When training is done right, how can it boost your company's productivity and bottom-line results?

Developing a Training Strategy

The smartest employers have fully embraced the fact that training (and development, which is discussed later in this chapter) requires a very deliberate, strategic, and focused set of initiatives. One of the first things any professional tasked with developing a training strategy for an organization must do is understand the short- and long-term strategies of the organization. And I'm not talking about a brief summary of where the organization *could* be in three to five to seven years. I'm talking about knowledge of the organization's growth plans, access to financial capital, and a thorough understanding of the human capital needs.

For example, let's say that a retailer such as Walgreens or CVS, whose stores seem to pop up on every block in America, has a growth strategy to open 500 stores domestically next year and 1,500 new stores in the next three years. If the average store has ten stockers, ten cashiers, three pharmacists, six pharmacy technicians, three photo techs, two loss-prevention personnel, five assistant managers, and one store manager, then each store requires forty people with at least eight different skill-sets. Even before accounting for normal attrition, Walgreens will need 2,000 new employees within a twelve-month period. And given that many of these new employees will not have received even the most basic of work skills from high school before entering the workplace, a thorough training program becomes mission-critical to the company's growth initiatives.

It would be silly and ill-advised for Walgreens or CVS to drop millions of dollars in brick-and-mortar stores when they are going to send untrained personnel in to provide shopping experiences to their customers, which is why the training professional must have a keen understanding of the organization's business plan in advance of attempting to devise a training strategy. From basic retailing concepts and profit-and-loss statements to safety and security issues, customer service skills, marketing, and community relations, the training initiatives must be all-encompassing and effective if the drugstore chain is going to have a shot at outpacing its competitors. Moreover, in the past, 60 percent of drugstore sales may have derived from the pharmacy and selling medications, but now many drugstore chains have diversified and sell groceries, greeting cards, furnishings, vitamins, nutritional supplements, gardening equipment—you name it. This training thing is serious business.

Now that the training professional has a strong grasp of where the organization is headed, the next step is figuring out exactly what kind of training is necessary. Here are step-by-step guidelines explaining how to develop a training strategy that suits your business, meets the needs of your employees, retains staff for as long as possible, and boosts your company's productivity.

Step 1: Assess Skills and Consider Preemployment Screening Tests

Many companies are turning to preemployment screening tests as a way to measure their applicants' skills and improve hiring. In fact, an American Management Association survey found that 44 percent of AMA members use these tests to select employees. Working with vendors, tests can be constructed to customize questions to suit your business. For example, Brinker International, which owns Chili's, On the Border, and other restaurant chains, tests whether future wait and service staff are reliable, friendly, and customer service oriented. A question—"Do you agree or disagree with the statement: If you can't say nice things, you shouldn't say anything at all?"—can reveal whether the applicant is going to offend people or be more sensitive to customers. These tests are one measure of assessing skills, and they are usually accompanied by interviews conducted by managers and other team members to provide a full picture of the applicant's strengths and weaknesses.

However, even these tests have their limitations. A January 7, 2009, article in *The Wall Street Journal* noted that Internet sites such as Vault.com provide inside tips on what these prescreening tests are looking for in each applicant, providing almost a "cheat sheet" on taking these tests.

Step 2: Develop Customized Training Based on Results of the Assessment

The success of any basic training program hinges on how well you can individualize the training to meet the needs of every employee. If you have tested staff adequately and diagnosed exactly what they need to round out their skills, you can develop specific training schedules, online training, internal courses, and external teaching for each employee. Cookie-cutter standard training for *all* staff is invariably less effective because it is more scattershot and not targeted to meet the needs of each employee.

Step 3: Use Various Methods of Delivering Training

Whether you are a small business or large corporation, training can be conducted in several ways, either online or one-on-one by having a new hire work alongside another employee on the job. In the old days, training only operated out of classrooms. Training has been transformed in the last few years by online options. Online training is fast and not overly expensive, and if you hire the right vendor, the training can be customized to suit your business's needs. One-on-one training, by definition, can be customized. So, for example, a newly hired member of your wait staff can shadow another waiter to observe how customer service is offered and to learn the difference between a Merlot and a rosé.

If you have employed pretesting to screen applicants, you can use the results to shape your training. If the applicants are weak in math, online training can improve their skills. If they have difficulty writing notes, online training can enhance those skills.

If only fifteen people work in every CVS or Walgreens on all shifts, removing the assistant manager for four weeks of intensive training may be too difficult. Customized online training can provide tools to prepare staff to become managers or assume other specialties. That training can be done within the store or on a laptop or computer at home, reducing the need to remove critical staff from the store for extended periods.

Other in-store strategies include mentoring with a manager or shadowing the manager or other specialists. Assistant managers can spend one or two days a week working closely with the manager and gaining valuable feedback. The assistant manager can run the store for a day under the watchful eye and tutelage of the manager.

In addition to using various methods of delivering training, companies usually need to offer training programs in specific areas or subjects that are critical to their business success. For example, your staff may need to master social etiquette skills or customer service know-how. Sometimes staff members must learn how to become adept in handling legal or media relations issues.

1. *Social Etiquette Training.* Increasingly, many staff members are coming to work not knowing the basics of work etiquette, including how to dress for work, how to take notes at a meeting, and the necessity of showing up for work and meetings on time. If a recently hired pharmaceutical sales representative doesn't know how to dress appropriately, or doesn't know what to discuss with the doctor during a one-on-one luncheon, the company's reputation can be damaged. Hence, social etiquette training may be as important for many staff members as basic writing and math training.

2. *Customer Service Training.* When American Express surveys its cardholders about restaurant dining, invariably the food and décor score high and the restaurant service is often lacking. A February 22, 2007, article in *Smart Money* magazine showed that customers with the highest customer satisfaction rates also boosted revenue.

   To retain top customers, win new ones, and avoid reputation risk, training to improve customer service staff is a necessity, not a luxury. Just as organizations provide specialized basic skills training, they can also provide online customer service training or classroom training geared to their industry. The more staff is trained to appeal to customers, the more sales are generated.

Remember, one size does not fit all in customer service. Most organizations recognize that 20 percent of customers generate 80 percent of their revenue, and these loyal and high-spending customers need to be treated differently than the occasional, penny-pinching client. Learning to differentiate between customers and treating them differently is essential to offering superior service. So, for example, if an airline reservation clerk receives a customer complaint from a Platinum frequent flyer who generates 100,000 miles of business, that customer may be offered a free domestic ticket to make up for the mistreatment. But the occasional customer, flying for the first time, could be offered a $25 discount certificate. Mastering customer service and differentiating between customers are all part of training. If an airline passenger in first-class has been drinking free liquor and gets inebriated and belligerent, how does an airline steward deal with that person most effectively? Since the airline faces liability issues, which can lead to a multimillion-dollar settlement if the passenger sues, handling these interactions successfully is very important. Designated training on how to handle difficult customers builds these skills, which often don't come naturally.

Instead of dealing with difficult customers in an "eye for eye" fashion ("the customer yelled at me, so I'll scream at the customer"), staff should be taught how to diffuse the conflict. Saying, "How can I help you and get you to your outcome?" shows customer sensitivity, whereas if your staff person responds by saying, "How dare you raise your voice at me? You have nerve," it will only anger the customer and likely lead to losing the customer forever. Some companies consider the life of the customer, so a loyal customer who buys a new Honda Accord every five years, for example, can generate $250,000 in revenue to an automobile manufacturer over twenty years. But staff must be trained to win customers over by sending them birthday cards, making follow-up calls, and treating them with respect, not disrespect.

Sunglass Hut (owned by Luxottica), for example, trains its employees to ask customers open-ended questions to ascertain why they want to buy a new set of sunglasses. In southern Florida and New York, for example, where tourists may number nearly half of all customers, store staff is taught how to be responsive to the needs of Europeans. The more Sunglass Hut's service reps can build rapport, get to know their customers, and select the right sunglasses for them, the more sales increase and loyal customers develop.

3. *Avoiding Liability Issues with Training.* Most organizations offer diversity training, so all members of the staff can be treated equitably and all customers can be treated with respect. All of these factors make good business sense. But there is another reason why diversity training is an imperative: avoiding liability and civil rights suits.

Managers, supervisors, and all staff members must be trained to treat all workers with respect, regardless of religion, race, or ethnicity. Staff must be given legal guidelines so that they can deal with other employees without transgressing any rules. How many times can a colleague ask someone on a date and get rejected before that employee can be accused of sexual harassment? Sexual harassment training is a necessary component of avoiding civil litigation. I've been at some companies where managers and supervisors pooh-pooh sexual harassment training. I've learned that the people who don't value and encourage this training are more than likely the ones to end up in the EEOC's office or a courtroom.

For example, if an employee says that she is a devout Christian and can't work on Sundays, when the organization needs Sunday coverage, does an employer have a right to compel the employee to work? Or is the employee obligated to work to meet the company's needs? Employees must be trained to handle these questions correctly and not trigger civil rights suits.

Or what if a person slips and falls in a retail store? Does the employee call 911? Contact the police? Take the injured person to a hospital or leave them alone? Does the employee know how to take notes in order to write an accurate accident report to limit the organization's liability? Only training prepares employees in the vital matters of avoiding costly and lengthy liability suits and protecting your customers and employees from aggravating any injury. If the employee hasn't been trained and fails to do the right thing, whose fault is that?

4. *Media Relations Training.* The media can influence and
    determine an organization's image and reputation. Many
    organizations, particularly smaller ones that don't have a
    public relations or media director or consultant to handle
    inquiries, leave dealing with the media to chance. That's
    a no-no. No matter if your organization has two employ-
    ees or thousands, staff should be trained to deal with a re-
    porter's call. When a customer service rep tells a reporter,
    "Oh, yeah, we got a lot of complaints on that product," it
    can ruin your company's reputation and sales.

    To deal with the media, staff needs to be trained on
    what to do when a reporter calls and how to handle the
    reporter's questions. If you are a larger organization and
    have a receptionist, that person must be trained to send
    the call to the proper person. "Please call our media rep-
    resentative, Shannon Smith, at the following number to
    ascertain whom you should contact," or "I'm not at lib-
    erty to answer your questions. Please call back when the
    owner/manager returns," are ways to handle a reporter's
    questions. If you have a website, designate a press contact
    to handle inquiries from reporters.

Match the Training with the Corporate Culture

If Wal-Mart is training managerial staff, it will develop a manager
who is utilitarian and focused on cost savings in order to fit into
the discount culture. Target, which has differentiated itself from
number-one retailer Wal-Mart by its emphasis on design and innovation, will train managers to be more visually inventive and imaginative. Nordstrom, which sets itself apart by its superior customer

service, develops people to specialize in meeting clients' needs. The training must fit the corporate culture and tie in with each company's competitive edge.

Training Boosts Retention—That's Why the U.S. Military Gets It

Most people want to be challenged; few want to stagnate. The more skills-building training you offer, the greater the chances you can retain people for a longer period. In *Field of Dreams*, Kevin Costner said, "Build it and they will come." In training lingo, train them and they will stay longer. If you teach staff new and challenging skills, the odds are better they will stay longer.

That catchy U.S. Army commercial, "Be All That You Can Be," exemplifies what the armed forces tries to accomplish in its training—and companies can learn from it. Many army recruits enlist for four years. And yet, despite that temporary stay, the U.S. Army trains recruits in useful skills needed to be radio technicians, computer experts, and repairmen. Offering college reimbursement serves as another way to retain soldiers by keeping them pumped and motivated over their four-year stay. The U.S. Army realizes that training keeps soldiers committed, renewed, and enlivened during their entire enlistment period.

A Fortune 500 Company Gets It

General Electric was ranked number six on the Fortune 500 list in 2008, based on $168 billion in revenue in 2007. Most companies can't match GE's resources. But part of the reason that GE has been adaptive to change is the resources it pours into its John F. Welch Leadership Center in Crotonville, NY. In fact, GE spends about $1 billion a year on training at its world-class learning center.

Bob Corcoran, GE chief learning officer, told *Training* magazine in a May 1, 2006, article "GE Hones Its Leaders at Crotonville" that "all of our major change initiatives—cultural change and business change processes—have either originated at Crotonville as a result of best practice assessments and evaluations or executive leadership summits, or they have been broadcast, trained, amplified, or rolled out with Crotonville as the change agent."

Other businesses can learn a variety of techniques from GE, despite not having the same financial resources to plunge into a learning center. For example:

1. To stay in business, change is necessary. Constantly search for new ways to reach customers, create new products, and test them out with customers.

2. At Crotonville, GE not only trains its senior leaders, but it invites customers to discuss its products and their future needs. Any organization could hold coffee klatches with its customers as a low-key, cost-efficient way to learn about customer needs.

3. In training sessions, GE staff members are assigned real problems that businesses face and must devise innovative solutions to them. Any entrepreneur could bring the staff together and have them problem-solve new solutions, just like GE does.

4. Mistakes are accepted. If a solution doesn't work, staff isn't punished. The idea is to test out new solutions and not chastise someone for making a mistake.

5. Besides focusing on business issues, participants discuss GE culture, what's working, what's not, and what can be improved. Having your staff discuss your organization's culture, what's working and what's not, can improve customer satisfaction and how your business operates.

6. Use any kind of learning, online or on-the-job, as a way to help staff deal with a changing business environment. What can we do differently? What can we do better? How can we appeal to new customers and retain our current ones?

Small Business Owners Get It

For many small businesses, delivering superior customer service isn't an add-on, an extra benefit, or the cherry on the sundae—it's about survival. Most small companies can't match industrial giants or retail superstores for promotional and advertising budgets. And they usually can't undersell the big guys. But they have one secret ingredient that can draw customers: superior customer service. But superior customer service skills can only be developed through training.

Paul Levesque, a customer service consultant, says that small businesses must train staff to "create one-on-one relationships to make their customers feel personally valued and appreciated in order to differentiate the small business from their competitors." Small businesses must create a "customer service culture" to succeed. For example, a customer comes into a hardware store and asks to find a wrench. At one store the sales clerk, who is reading a newspaper, points to the back of the store. At another store, the clerk says, "Let me escort you to exactly where the wrench is. And is there anything else I can help you with today?" At the second store, the clerk knows that "taking care of the customer is more important than any other task," Levesque notes. That clerk was trained in one-on-one sessions to make customer service a priority.

Building a customer service culture starts with the owner/operator. If the owner is rude, the staff will usually adopt that attitude. If the owner makes customer service priority number one, staff follows. Entrepreneurs can model behavior, hold staff meetings before work, explain how clerks can deal with negative customers and turn them around, and train staff one-on-one.

At Weber's Restaurant, a hamburger eatery in Orillia, Ontario, about seventy-five miles north of Toronto, the owners invite employees to constantly devise ways to please customers. When one server started singing the 1960s classic "Duke of Earl" when he was serving customers, it caught on, and now many servers sing it or other do-wop songs. It has become one of the signature experiences at Weber's. Another employee saw seniors getting tired when standing on line. He suggested that the owner buy benches. Now seniors sit and don't mind waiting longer. Training staff to be part of a customer service culture often leads to higher revenue.

The Biggest Obstacle to Great Training Initiatives

Most companies make the most critical mistake when they don't fully support training a hundred percent. When employees know that the CEO and the organization are fully committed to training and that training is essential to the organization's growth, then everyone takes it seriously. When the CEO holds employees accountable for training and stresses and reinforces its importance, then everyone is on board. CEOs must treat training as mission-critical to the organization.

For training to thrive, organizations must view it as part of their business strategy. Just as developing a marketing campaign is part of a business strategy, so is developing the skills of the staff.

Often, however, the CEO gives training lip service. If the CEO describes the company as a learning organization and only provides empty rhetoric, allowing managers to remove people from training when an all-too-important deadline is near, then everyone knows training is secondary and an afterthought. When you hear the CEO say training is the right thing to do at the annual staff meeting and then forgets about it for the rest of the year, few will take training seriously.

Your employees will know if the company is doing training because it is supposed to, not because the organization truly supports it. For example, some companies treat sexual harassment or diversity training like a necessary evil, rather than explaining why it is imperative that everyone is properly trained about these issues. When I was an HR executive at Blockbuster, I knew there was staff resistance to sexual harassment training. To counteract the resentment, I asked each Blockbuster business manager to send a personal note to the staff attending training to inform them that in the previous year Blockbuster spent X amount of dollars in attorney fees for sexual harassment cases that might otherwise have added thousands of dollars to their bonuses. That simple note sent a very strong message that sexual harassment courses matter and that everyone on staff should attend, pay attention, and follow the guidelines.

Developing Leaders

As previously stated, training involves improving someone's skills in an existing job, whereas leadership development entails preparing the senior leaders of your organization in the future. Here are the key steps that an organization needs to take to develop a leadership strategy.

Step 1: Assess Your Current Leadership

The first thing you need to do is study your leadership chart, identifying who your top leaders are and assessing your bench strength—that is, your next line of people who could succeed your top leaders if they were to depart. Many companies engage in an exercise where the senior-most people assess the top twenty-five critical positions that the company couldn't do without. That list will differ from organization to organization. At Coca-Cola, the staff who guard the beverage's secret formula would likely surface in the top twenty-five. At Procter & Gamble, marketing staff would be included, whereas at Countrywide Financial, before Bank of America's acquisition, it might be the financial and risk managers trying to save the company.

After the senior managers have identified the top twenty-five people, they name the next 150 people that the organization couldn't live without. These people are the next tier of invaluable contributors to the company. Usually you name no more than 5 percent of the company's top echelon because it's unwieldy dealing with more than that number.

Next, we develop a replacement plan for each of these 150 people. We focus on the people most likely to leave in twelve, eighteen, and twenty-four months. Who were the likely replacements? Who on staff had the skills to immediately step in as a replacement? If there was someone on staff who was promising but not fully developed yet, then we'd devise a leadership plan (see step 2). If nobody was ready, senior managers look outside the company, study competitors, and attend conferences to identify suitable replacements.

Step 2: Develop a Customized Leadership Plan

You can't make leaders the same way you make a pan of cupcakes. Leaders don't fit into a mold. Each person has unique and specific needs, strengths, and weaknesses and therefore requires a customized leadership plan to close any skills gaps and provide the skills that are lacking.

For example, if you were devising a leadership plan for your controller who was being considered as the next CFO, you'd note that the controller has not handled quarterly analysts' calls. The HR executive might suggest that the CFO start to bring the controller along to the quarterly calls and walk him through how they prepare—how they predict the questions that will be asked, handle the numbers, and deal with aggressive and inquisitive reporters (are there any other kind?). On-the-job training fills in and can serve as the best kind of preparation in this situation.

Since the controller had not previously worked at a publicly traded company, he might be sent to classes at the American Management Association on handling Sarbanes-Oxley and other SEC disclosure rules. In addition, since the controller manages ten people and the CFO oversees 150 people, the controller might spend a week at the Center for Creative Leadership identifying his management style and learning or refining leadership techniques needed to oversee a much larger staff.

One other strategy that has proved particularly effective for training future leaders is sending them to executive MBA programs. Weekend, summer, and occasionally after-work MBA programs usually take three years to complete and are paid by the company. If the employee leaves the company early—that is, before at least three years or until the MBA program is completed—she may be required to reimburse the organization, which serves as a real stimulus for the employee to stay for a minimum of three years. Moreover, since the company has exerted so much confidence in the person, it often serves as a stimulus to stay longer, beyond completing the degree.

Step 3: Choose Leaders Who Fit the Culture

In 2001 or so, Apple Computer was hurting. Sales were down, its culture seemed to be fading, and innovation was dormant. Apple was known for producing hardware and was considered just another computer manufacturer like IBM and Dell. Then it decided that in order to be competitive, it must innovate or die. Apple hired a leadership team that was dedicated to change. It adapted to a new culture and proceeded to have one success after another.

Apple's management team was open to breaking boundaries, creating new products, and truly thinking outside the box—and, more specifically, outside the traditional laptop design. The results were skyrocketing revenue and a series of groundbreaking products, from iPods to iPhones.

Moreover, although Apple had faced failures with two projects, it didn't deter CEO Steve Jobs from sustaining the spirit of innovation at the company. Jim Pinto, a business writer at Automation.com, a news Internet site, wrote, "At Apple, there is no micromanagement; responsibility is pushed down; talented people are let loose." Another noted that to launch the iPod, Apple invoked several types of innovation, including networking (forging an inventive agreement among music companies to license their songs online), business models (songs sold for a buck each), and branding (based on sleek, svelte product designs).

Step 4: Choose Leaders Who Exemplify Company Values

Choosing leaders isn't just about selecting the best engineer, marketer, or designer; it's about developing people who exemplify the company's core values. If you choose a corrupt financial whiz who is aggressive but used to cutting corners, treating people shabbily, and not playing by the rules, the company suffers. Arthur Andersen, WorldCom, and Enron were once companies that had multibillion-dollar revenues, but when the CEOs and senior management teams acted unethically, it led to the demise of each company. Choose people for leadership programs that retain the company's core principles and culture.

Step 5: Choose Leaders Who Exhibit Multiple Characteristics

As stated, it is not always the best accountant who becomes the next CFO. Leadership to manage 100 people requires more complex skills than mastering Finance 101 and the general ledger. In *Good to Great*, Jim Collins noted that "leaders are the most important element in moving organizations from average to excellent, and leadership consists of several elements, including building a strong organization, courageous leadership, building an adaptive organizational culture, and fostering creative innovation." Collins suggests that the best engineer doesn't necessarily advance to leading people and becoming a manager. It takes a different skill-set to become a leader than mastery of one's profession.

Look at who becomes the executive director of a hospital. Often the person in charge of every element of a hospital isn't a trained medical doctor but an administrator who has climbed the ladder through operations and management, mastered finance and budgeting, and knows how to train people and choose leaders.

Proving Collins's point that leadership requires an array of skills, not just one dominant trait, was the decision that IBM made in choosing Louis Gerstner as CEO in 1993. Gerstner had been CEO of RJR Nabisco and previously had been a senior executive at American Express and McKinsey & Company. Scuttlebutt was that he used a computer but knew as much about them as any layman. IBM wasn't seeking a computer whiz; if it were, it would not have hired Gerstner.

In 1993, IBM's mainframe business had lost its vigor and faced declining sales. IBM executives knew that the business had to be reengineered or turned around or it could fade in the future. It hired Gerstner for his management skills and innovative practices, not his computer know-how. Gerstner decided to focus on IBM's IT services business and used the Internet, which was just beginning to expand, as the cornerstone of the business. By the time Gerstner left IBM in 2002, after nearly a decade as its CEO, IT services constituted nearly 50 percent of IBM's income. IBM's selection of Gerstner proved that the selection of a CEO should be based on multiple skills, character, and innovation, not one limited and specific skill-set.

Tips from an Experienced Leadership and Development Expert

In his last four positions as vice president of employee learning at LendingTree, organizational development manager at Heineken USA, training and development manager at DoubleClick, and global sales training director at Avon Products, Edward Van Luinen has played a key leadership and training role at each of those companies. Van Luinen, who is based in Pasadena, CA, runs his own eponymous consulting company. Here are his tips on how companies can effectively develop a training and leadership strategy.

Tip 1: Connect with the Business Strategy

Van Luinen says the overriding factor in developing a training agenda is connecting training with the business strategy. Since strategies are changing so rapidly, most companies review training initiative annually in order to alter and update the training. For example, when he was at Avon Products, the company introduced a new sales approach to boost revenue. To help fine-tune training, he had to be knowledgeable about Avon's business model, its revenue streams, and how salespeople operated in order to design training that would improve skills. Since much of Avon's sales approach revolved around understanding the customer better, training provided new ways to meet customer needs, anticipate them, and deliver stronger results.

Tip 2: Develop a Group of Business Leaders Who Support Training

In order for training to be effective, it requires credibility in the organization and the support of senior management. That support sends a message that training is aligned with the company's business strategy. To provide this credibility, Van Luinen created a learning council of business leaders who help develop and suggest training and serve as training enthusiasts and "evangelists." They also serve as a "reality check" to suggest any changes in training as the business strategy changes.

Tip 3: Know Your Training Staff and Consultants

Despite the movement toward e-learning, most management and leadership training still relies on internal trainers and external consultants to teach courses and workshops. Knowing the strengths and weaknesses of the internal and external teaching staff enables the training development staff to more effectively develop courses that fit the trainer's abilities.

Tip 4: Assess the Staff's Strengths and Weaknesses

When Van Luinen was at DoubleClick, a global Internet advertising solutions company, he concentrated on performing a gap or needs analysis of the sales staff to determine what skills each staff member possessed and what skills were lacking. He interviewed many of the sales staff and their managers to determine what skills were lacking, then developed training courses to fill in those voids. "The gap analysis became the basis for DoubleClick's training programs," he says.

Tip 5: Connect the Training to the Culture

Avon's culture revolves around developing strong, lasting relationships with customers. Building that relationship requires highly interactive dealings with the customers. Hence, training at Avon stressed interactive learning—that is, providing feedback to the teacher and feedback to students mirroring the sales/customer rapport. Van Luinen describes this interactive learning as consisting of role-playing interspersed with action learning teams solving business problems. "Culture has a huge impact on how training is organized," asserts Van Luinen.

Tip 6: Use Training to Boost Retention

When organizations devote time, budgets, and energy to training, it sends a positive message that the business is investing resources into improving the skills of its staff members. Training enhances job satisfaction and boosts retention. Many companies that Van Luinen developed training strategies for used training as a way to boost skills and strengthen ties to employees, leading to longer retention and less turnover.

Tip 7: Decide on One of Three Approaches to Training

Having developed training and leadership strategies and programs at several organizations, Van Luinen says that companies often employ one of three training approaches: (1) Some companies invest in training in good and bad times and use training to boost sales, improve marketing, and develop innovative products when revenues lag. (2) Other organizations invest in training, but the minute a downturn occurs, they cut back, reduce classes, and keep staff back in the field and focused on sales, curtailing time spent in training. (3) Some organizations avoid training in good times and bad. As a training professional, Van Luinen obviously contends that the organizations that sustain training in good and bad times come out ahead.

Tip 8: Create Ways for HR to Partner with Business Managers

When Van Luinen was at LendingTree, HR and business managers partnered to create a strategy to boost staff retention. HR and business managers met biweekly and focused on how to recruit salespeople and, once hired, keep them. Having business managers partner with HR was critical since the business managers are primarily responsible for each salesperson's development and appraisals. The results of this cross-function effort was turnover at Lending Tree was reduced by 8 percent. When he was at DoubleClick, discussions focused on how to prepare newly hired staff so they would hit the ground running, and then coaching was used to enhance and improve their sales skills after they were hired. Van Luinen attributes the ability to retain staff to "sales coaching, feedback, rewards, recruiting, and training."

Tip 9: Use E-learning to Reduce Training Costs but Provide an Invaluable Service

Classroom training can be very expensive since often consultants have to be hired. It is also time-consuming for staff because it takes them away from the office and normal duties. When Van Luinen was at DoubleClick, he developed an extensive e-learning program for the IT staff. The training helped IT staff gain certification, improve customer service skills, and enhance their problem-solving abilities. Staff members could train on their own time, and each learning module included testing to ensure that skills were mastered. Van Luinen describes the advantages of e-learning as "providing low-cost training, economies of scale, and an ability for staff to measure their own success online." E-learning is particularly effective with Generation Xers and the Millennial who were raised on computers; some baby boomers have a more difficult time with online training, while others take easily to it. He also notes that some classes, particularly in management and leadership, are better taught through a classroom setting and not online. Some classes, like conflict resolution and some writing courses, for example, require the in-classroom guidance of a teacher.

Tip 10: Choose the Appropriate Leadership Strategy That Fits the Company

At DoubleClick, Van Luinen discussed the company's leadership strategy with the CEO. The CEO faced a choice of instituting a strategy that either focused on sharing a vision with the staff, which meant learning how to communicate the strategy to the staff, or a strategy that stressed self-development. Because DoubleClick was involved in Internet marketing and advertising, which was changing rapidly, the CEO felt strongly that the only way to build an effective leadership program was to focus on self-development. By the time the staff member learned what the vision was and how to communicate it, the vision would change. Furthermore, DoubleClick tended to hire junior staff members and promote them quickly, so stressing self-development made the most sense when it came to training its more inexperienced managers for leadership positions. Van Luinen also introduced executive coaching, which offered personalized assistance and leadership growth. DoubleClick's program reinforced that leadership training must fit into the organization's culture and tie in with its business strategy in order to be successful.

Tip 11: Avoid the Trap of Creating Training That Doesn't Fit the Job

When training most often receives negative feedback, it stems from the courses not being pertinent or germane to the person's actual job. Often this oversight is attributable to HR's not doing strong enough needs assessments of what exactly the person in the job does and what training is required to update the person's skills.

If the training manager uses the job description and focuses on the job's competencies, training is more aligned with what the job actually does and where the person needs to grow.

In short, if training is done extensively and executed effectively, it can serve as the secret ingredient to retaining employees. Employees who are challenged, motivated, and learn new skills stay. Those who are bored, stuck, feel trapped, and keep repeating the same tasks look for new opportunities. If done right, training is another way to build loyalty and increase retention while developing your leaders for the future. It's a true win-win.

CHAPTER SIX

♦ ♦ ♦

WHAT YOU SHOULD EXPECT FROM YOUR HR EXECUTIVE

Fast Company's July 2006 cover story, "Why We Hate HR," was its highest-selling issue of the year. Everyone, it seems, has a grievance against HR. HR doesn't treat us right. HR doesn't do its job capably. HR makes us submit hordes of unnecessary paperwork and forms. And HR forces us to do performance appraisals. The complaints go on and on. Blaming HR for making mistakes has become a cliché in corporate America. And yet, whose fault is it that HR engenders so much antipathy? Is HR itself to blame, or have business leaders created a no-win situation for HR by giving it a myriad of responsibilities and little autonomy? Most important, what can be done to turn HR into a force that helps the company increase revenue and improve productivity rather than serving as a punching bag for everyone's scathing criticisms?

Where has HR gone wrong? As Elizabeth Barrett Browning might have written in a poem, let me count the ways. Here are the four major issues I see with HR.

Issue 1: Know HR

The first problem in HR going awry stems from the people that CEOs and senior executives select to lead HR. Organizations often choose HR executives who meet much lower standards than those executives selected for senior financial, sales, marketing, and other leadership positions. There's a maxim in business school that the A and B students choose investment banking, finance, and marketing, and the C students settle for HR. For too long, organizations have been satisfied with C students running HR, people they would never tolerate in revenue-producing areas.

It wasn't too long ago that many HR leaders didn't even possess undergraduate degrees. In some organizations, enterprising administrative assistants climbed the corporate ladder and were named HR top executive. Imagine the head of HR, someone running a fifty-person department with a several million-dollar budget, influencing an entire multimillion-dollar operation without formal training? Would the CEO select a former bookkeeper to lead the finance team? Doubtful. Would the executive team opt for someone to lead marketing who had made a couple of cold calls without a strong track record of success and an outstanding resume? Doubtful. But the HR top executive may be someone without formal education who has dabbled in HR and knows little about recruiting, HR strategy, HR theory, and HR practices. When the CEO says that the most important asset in our organization is the people, and then hires a mediocre employee without any formal education to lead HR, something is out of sync.

If people are really the organization's major asset, then the leader of HR must reflect that and be an A-list player. The HR top executive can choose talent, influence and shape recruitment, develop people, retain the best people, and serve as a difference maker in the organization's future. But at many companies, it would require a mental shift for most business people to view HR in a new light and as a force to be reckoned with.

If the person hired to be an HR senior executive is not the most dynamic leader, the best talent evaluator, the person who can motivate and lead, then the HR function is going to falter. CEOs can't choose a second-rate person to perform some of the most complex tasks in the organization—tasks that include identifying the right people, surmounting the competition to hire the best staff, creating a strategy that rewards people, and developing the best training and leadership programs. Hiring second-rate people to lead HR is a recipe for disaster. No wonder so many people are antagonistic toward HR. If the HR leader is ill equipped to perform the job, I blame the CEO and leadership team for not respecting HR and selecting the most qualified and best candidate for the job.

Many CEOs say they value HR, but in reality, HR is viewed as a second cousin, an afterthought, a "soft skill," an extra added function, a cost center, not a revenue producer. Too many CEOs don't see the connection between the influence and power that HR can wield in selecting the most imaginative staff, the innovative thinkers, the future leaders, and its ability to help an organization generate revenue. If an HR senior executive selects a talented leader to be CEO of a subsidiary and that subsidiary generates millions of dollars in revenue, the CEO takes credit for choosing that leader and expanding revenue streams. How many

CEOs would acknowledge that the HR senior executive and the HR team were instrumental in identifying the talent and leading the interviews and were ultimately responsible for the hiring?

One of the HR senior executive's main missions is making sure the organization makes people its most important asset. If a CEO or senior management team chooses the wrong, poorly informed HR senior executive to lead the recruiting and hiring team, it is equivalent to a bus company choosing a driver who can't steer the vehicle.

Just as the general counsel of the firm needs to have a strong legal background and the CFO requires advanced finance education, so must the HR leader possess a strong background in HR practices. There is an organized body of knowledge that must be learned and mastered, just as there is in other disciplines such as law or finance. But many CEOs think that understanding human nature is intuitive, that an HR manager can rely on instincts, gut reaction, and observation, rather than have formal knowledge. HR leaders must know about compensation, negotiation, recruiting, benefits, retention, and motivation, and those concepts are just a starting point.

The effects of hiring an incompetent HR executive are felt on the bottom line. When senior HR executives of an airline negotiate long-term contracts with pilots that obligate the airline to pay 10 percent annual increases in base pay, at a time when fuel prices are escalating and airlines are losing millions of dollars, HR has forced that company into a labor nightmare. Even though CEOs use the patronizing term *soft skill* to describe what HR does, in most cases HR decisions affect revenue, income, and profit. There's really nothing soft about it.

When I transferred from the general counsel's office to become HR executive at Blockbuster., I concentrated on gaining and learning the HR body of knowledge. Just as I studied for the bar exam, I took time to master HR practices by gaining certification from the Human Resource Certification Institute. I read books, reviewed the academic scholarship on HR, took a prep course, then took and passed the formal exam, proving that I had mastered the HR body of knowledge. Before becoming the HR executive, I wanted to make sure that I had the HR expertise needed to support my decisions. After gaining that certification, I also took follow-up continuing education courses, just as attorneys are required to take continuing education courses to upgrade their knowledge. In short, knowing HR leads to effectively practicing HR. If the HR leader doesn't possess the body of knowledge and expertise to answer these nuts-and-bolts questions, business leaders rightfully *don't* and *shouldn't* respect HR.

Issue 2: Do HR

The job of HR executive is extremely complex because it entails two very different, but equally important, tasks. One function of the job involves bread-and-butter issues, like paying people, making sure healthcare benefits are paid, and overseeing employee relations—what I refer to as keeping the trains running on time. Everyone takes these everyday tasks for granted until an employee is not paid or a parent takes her child to the emergency room and the hospital fails to recognize the employee's health plan. Most people complain about HR when something goes wrong. But when everything goes right and the trains are running on time, no one goes out of their way to compliment HR for doing a good job. Talk about a no-win situation.

The second function entails making complicated, strategic decisions about what kind of personnel the firm needs in the future, creating an approach to hiring them, connecting people with business revenue, and devising ways to keep people for as long as possible. Performing the second function of creating an HR strategy involves knowing the business and its future outlook. All of that strategic thinking depends on working closely with the organization's leaders.

Issue 3: Align HR

The overlooked part of the HR job is strategic. Which employees must be hired to stay competitive in the next decade? How does the organization choose employees who will move the company forward? How can the organization retain staff when competitors are offering more creative compensation and reward packages? How can we expand our sales force overseas? How do we find the most creative MBAs to hire, not just bureaucrats? If we are opening lines of business that generate new revenue streams, how can we hire people quickly and yet maintain the highest standards? All of these business-related questions are complex and demand sophisticated HR responses.

To answer all these questions, HR must be aligned with business units and must work collaboratively with them to be on the same wavelength. In the past, HR leaders and business leaders would lay out their strategy and future plans separately. *HR leaders* would have an offsite meeting and establish a list of eight major initiatives that they hoped to accomplish in the coming year. Separately, the *business leaders* (finance, sales, marketing, operations) would go offsite and create their eight major initiatives intended to boost revenue in the coming year. When the business leaders looked at the HR leaders' initiatives, they would pooh-pooh them and not see the value in helping HR accomplish their business goals. This misalignment is often at the root of disagreement between HR and business. Unless HR and the businesses work cohesively at the outset, problems arise.

What I find surprising about the misalignment is that in almost every business, personnel costs are the number-one line item. It's not rent, electricity, or supplies that constitute the highest cost, but salaries. Hence, if people are our most important asset and people are the most expensive cost center in the business, then aligning business with HR, which oversees hiring and personnel costs, makes the most sense—but this rarely happens.

Who is responsible for this misalignment? Really it doesn't matter; the point is that HR and the business must fix the problem. HR must take a leadership role, reach out to business units, and convince the businesses that it can assist in hiring the right people if it understands future business strategies and growth plans. But businesses must also recognize that HR has the expertise in recruiting and hiring employees and therefore can add value.

Issue 4: Assess HR

Measurement and assessment are two different concepts. You measure activity; you assess outcomes. Too many HR departments are reluctant to assess programs and initiatives. If HR initiates a new customer service program and requires 500 employees to undergo training, HR sends out a report that 500 people were trained for four hours, costing the company $240,000. That's measurement. But assessment focuses on whether the program was effective and produced a return on investment. Did the customer service training improve revenue, bring in new customers, and raise satisfaction levels?

Defensive and afraid to be evaluated, HR often eschews assessment and pays a price for never knowing whether its programs are truly effective. Ironically, most business people recognize that some programs are going to fail, but you have to take risks and launch them anyway. HR people, on the other hand, are loath to launch an initiative if it has any risk of failing. Lacking confidence in their place in the organization, many HR departments are running scared and afraid to assess their efforts.

Hiring decisions, which are so critical to every organization's performance, often aren't evaluated to determine why they succeeded or failed. If a new CFO is hired after a six-month or year-long search and leaves within six months, that departure can cost the company hundreds of thousands of dollars. Why didn't the CFO fit into the organization? Was the CFO lacking finance or human relations skills? What questions weren't asked that should have been? What red flags in the CFO's resume or recommendations might have been missed? What can the organization learn from the CFO's quick departure to ensure that this hiring mistake doesn't happen again?

Several years ago, HR endured a metrics frenzy. To shore up their position and stature in the organization, HR departments produced hundreds of pages of metric studies on all sorts of subjects. Unfortunately, most of those studies offered self-serving, inside HR statistics that fulfilled no purpose other than to fill many binders that collected dust on the HR bookshelf. HR needs to evaluate its efforts and make sure that it is not only measuring but assessing what the business actually needs to know.

Forming a New Business/HR Collaboration

HR cannot operate on one track and business on another, like two train tracks that will never cross. Once HR masters the complexities of HR and aligns with businesses, a new collaboration can form where, together, HR and the business create a dynamic duo. In simplest terms, business understands the value of HR, and HR recognizes its role in helping the business realize its goals. In addition, HR recognizes the important value it can add to the business.

No longer will HR operate as the defensive, half-hearted afterthought; instead, it will be a major contributor to identifying staff, training them, and retaining them. No longer will business scoff, denigrate, and malign HR, but will consider it an equal partner. If people are the most important asset of any company, then HR plays a major role in the organization by hiring the right people. Moreover, other business leaders must recognize HR's impact on the bottom line.

Publicizing HR's Efforts

In the past, HR was often reluctant to publicize its efforts. Huddled in the background, HR would take reams of criticism for nearly anything that went awry, but if something went right, some other department seized the credit. HR must learn to champion its own efforts and announce its victories. If HR played a role in hiring the new CEO of a subsidiary that is generating millions of dollars in revenue, the HR executive should let other senior managers know. Success breeds success. By publicizing its efforts, HR can begin to alter the negative perceptions others in the company have about HR. When *Fast Company* writes a follow-up story on how "Everyone Respects HR," then HR will have come full circle and entered a new arena.

Going from Business Partner to Part of the Business

For a long time, HR leaders talked about becoming partners with the business. Whenever I attended an HR meeting, partnering with business became a mantra. But there's a major problem with HR leaders who constantly strive to join their business as partners because they are still considered outside of the business. Striving to become a partner is like someone constantly asking to be considered an equal. If you are truly equal, you sit at the table, exert influence, and don't have to ask to be a partner. You *are* part of the business.

The first step for any HR leader is to build relationships in order to be considered a trusted business partner. The business is your client. But it's not enough just to be a business partner. Over time the relationship must evolve into that of an equal, where HR is *part* of the business, not just a *partner* to the business. That's when HR knows it's at the top of its game.

HR is part of the business when it is recognized as the expert in human resources matters, just as the CFO specializes in finance and the general counsel knows legal issues. HR has a seat at the table because it has the facts on retention, hiring the best people, establishing a long-term hiring strategy, dealing with compensation and healthcare issues, the list goes on and on. It doesn't have to strive, influence, and cajole to convince the business to become a partner. If HR is to be effective, successful, and recognized for creating value, it has to be involved and immersed in every business decision. If it is outside of the business and then told later about future growth strategies and plans, problems and disruptions follow.

In the late 1990s, theme parks were the craze on Wall Street. Paramount Pictures, Six Flags, and Universal Studios were riding the economic wave and expanding the out-of-home entertainment market. During this period, the economy was so strong that unemployment dipped below 2 percent in many areas of the country. And many labor experts quipped that because 3 percent of the population does not want to work anyway, employers were now going to have spend time convincing people to work who didn't otherwise want to! Notwithstanding the limited access to labor, theme park business management teams continued to create ambitious and rapid expansion plans. This is how it went: The business leaders would go into a room and meet and decide to grow their theme park businesses because they had customer demand and access to financial capital. I dare say most—if not all—of those *planning* meetings did not include HR, although ultimately HR was going to be tasked with finding all of those bright, smiling, customer-centric employees necessary to staff a park. They would leave the room and hold a big press conference with the media and investment community, proclaiming their next major initiative or BHAG (Big Hairy Audacious Goal, a term coined by Jim Collins, author of *Good to Great*).

The HR leaders, who oftentimes first learned of these plans when everyone else did, would sit there in shock, asking themselves how their business leaders could make these decisions without taking into account one very important issue: There was insufficient human capital to make their dreams or business ventures come true.

Having served as one of those HR executives during that period and in that industry, I (as the HR leader) was forced to battle with my business leader colleagues who felt the HR team was not working hard enough and/or was not smart enough to satisfy their insatiable needs for talent. I often had to remind them that it was *they* who met and decided to expand a business without having a conversation with *me* about how *we* would staff the business. I spent countless hours explaining how difficult it is to find good people to work in relatively low-paying, seasonal, non-benefit-eligible jobs. My team developed several proposals that included busing people from miles away at great expense and pursuing visas for foreign visitors to supplement the domestic workforce, which would take time (they called that un-business-friendly and "characteristically HR"). The moral here is if only the business leaders had involved the HR leaders at the outset in the spirit of a real business partnership, the problem would have been solved.

In essence, HR could have helped the theme park executives in three ways. First, had HR been brought in on the front end, it could have worked with the management team to develop a feasible hiring and development timeline. HR would tell management how long it takes to recruit the type of employees sought. Even if the company had obtained financial capital, we might have asked for a delayed opening based on the lack of access to human capital. In fact, when unemployment is at 2 percent, as it was in the late 1990s, sometimes HR can advise not to move forward with expansion plans. Second, if the plan was moving forward, HR could have developed a staffing strategy that brought in quality inexpensive workers from outside of the United States on temporary work visas to help staff the new parks. Obtaining a work visa is complicated and time-consuming, but this approach can work for larger employers such as theme park operators. Finally, if HR had been consulted in the planning and development process, it could have recommended ways to operate more efficiently and with fewer staff. Had HR been consulted on park design and retail operations (e.g., which types of point-of-sale equipment would be easier for unskilled workers to use, what types of products could be sold with the fewest number of employees), it could have devised a more thoughtful hiring plan to meet the target opening dates. The entire business concept of Disney's EPCOT, for example, is predicated on finding native people to represent a "real-life world" experience.

Why HR Must Sit at the Table

If people are the organization's most important asset, then HR, the expert on people issues, must sit at the table, get involved in decision making, offer its expertise, and be inextricably involved in any decision that affects staffing. If it's not, HR is not operating at maximum capacity.

And some business leaders are going to have to overcome their resistance to making HR a part of the business. I've seen executives display three possible reactions to making HR a true business partner: (1) Some business executives actively despise the idea. They've considered HR managers as subordinates for years, don't want to make any adjustments, don't understand HR's role, and resent HR sitting at the table with them. (2) Other executives begrudgingly accept HR as a partner but consider it a necessary evil, like having to go to the dentist to fix a cavity. It's necessary but painful. But these executives at least know enough to bring HR into meetings and to consider their view, and albeit reluctantly, they depend on HR's expertise. (3) Enlightened business executives welcome HR as an equal participant. Knowing that HR possesses expertise that they don't have, these progressive leaders depend on HR to offer insight into their future plans, help recruit and retain employees, and build revenue growth together.

The business executives who fight to keep HR out of meetings and keep them at a distance are operating in a myopic, shortsighted universe. They are like a couple that has bought land to build a house, hired a contractor, started building the foundation, ordered the bricks, and then hires an architect to design the house. If the house is to be built properly, the architect must be in on the ground floor, literally and figuratively, not brought in after the foundation has been constructed. Similarly, if the business is to run effectively, HR must also get involved at the beginning and on every business strategy.

In the past, part of the resistance to getting HR more involved in the business has been the fact that CEOs and senior managers and nearly everyone else thinks that they are experts in people. Most business executives think, "I know people, I know talent, I know which people to hire." I think these senior managers are misinformed. In my view, business people who fail to rely on HR are like the guy with back pain who refuses to go to a doctor because he says he knows his body better than anyone else. Instead of gaining the expertise of a medical specialist, the stubborn individual self-diagnoses and ends up never getting rid of his back pain.

Why HR Has to Make Changes, Too

But it's not just business executives who have to make a mental shift. HR must also make changes when it becomes immersed in business dealings. At the beginning of this chapter, I made the point that HR must know, do, and assess in order to align with businesses. HR must have the statistics on retention; it must know the talent that is available, keep abreast of employment trends, attend business conferences, and be as well versed on current staffing issues as physicians are on changing medical conditions and attorneys are on new verdicts.

Furthermore, HR people have to truly feel empowered. They must know they can make a difference, believe in their strengths, operate as full partners, and be as committed to success as the business leaders are. In fact, that reminds me of an HR leader I met recently. I had just given a speech on HR having a sit at the table, and she told me how she appreciated my message and how she was going to work hard to change HR's influence at her company.

But when I asked what she expected to do differently to make this happen, she said she needed to convince the CEO why HR deserved a seat at the table. What she said made sense, but her tone was equivocal and unsure, as if she was trying to convince herself. I stopped her and said, "With all due respect, you don't sound as if you truly believe you belong at the table. It sounds as if you're trying to convince yourself that you belong there. If you don't truly feel it and believe it, you're never going to convince your CEO." She agreed that I was right. The point is, HR must feel totally empowered on its own. HR must know its stuff, possess the facts, do its homework, and devise studies on retention and exits in order to be considered expert.

When HR Is Firing on All Cylinders

When HR gains the trust of the business and the employees, suddenly it's as if they can't do without HR. When HR is effective, knowledgeable, initiating, and tuned in, businesses won't even consider holding a meeting *without* HR. HR is a part of the business. HR is the trusted confidant, talent finder, business strategist, retention expert, health benefits expert, and training specialist. Once the business trusts HR and relies on its judgment, HR becomes inextricably involved in all parts of the business. Moreover, the business isn't going out of its way to invite HR to participate, but accepts that HR is critical to getting the job done.

If HR is doing its job well, recruiting the best people, attracting the best talent, and grooming staff, the company is building a reputation as an employer of choice. While HR may not get much overt credit and may operate mostly behind the scenes, it is in the forefront of establishing an organization as one of the most desired companies in the industry to work for. In the 1980s and early 1990s, when Southwest Airlines was one of the fastest-growing carriers in the nation, it didn't have to take out ads to attract people. The company's reputation for creating a great culture, paying people fairly, and treating people equitably established it as an employer of choice. Again, HR played a lead role in helping create this culture of hard work, advancement, fun, and equitable payment. Southwest became a talent magnet due to its dynamic culture and having an empowered HR organization contribute to that culture.

Furthermore, when HR is playing the lead role in hiring, recruiting, developing, and grooming talent, management can spend less time on HR activities such as hiring and retaining talent and more time on sales and marketing. Finance can focus on the balance sheet, marketing on selling and creating new products, and IT on technology. HR concentrates on its core strength, which is people, and the business areas can focus their expertise on boosting revenue.

When HR Is Effective, Retention Rises

When HR is doing its job to its maximum and hiring the best and brightest people, the energy created at the company has a life of its own. Most smart people want to work with other intelligent individuals, not a staff of cynics or indifferent workers. Granted, most people these days are going to leave even an exceptional company in four or five years, but the organizations where HR is operating on all cylinders retain people for longer periods. Rather than looking to skip out after two years, people last four years or more.

By hiring the best people, HR can target the four or five "superstars" it wants to develop into its future leaders. Just as General Electric became a training ground for future CEOs, the organizations where HR shines can become leaders in developing its future leaders.

What HR Must Do to Become an Integral Part of Business

The two words that spring to mind that establish HR as an integral part of an organization are credibility and relationships. Once HR establishes its reputation of knowing its material, living up to expectations, delivering the goods, and understanding issues from a business perspective, it gains credibility. Credibility is also based on establishing strong relationships with business leaders. Once they know and trust you and see that HR can help advance their business, the rapport grows and the business depends on HR.

New Roles for HR to Perform

When HR is operating at maximum capacity and has proved its mettle and value to business leaders, it is viewed as a revenue producer, not a cost center. When an HR executive of a Fortune 500 organization manages 500 people and oversees a budget of $70 million, he is charged with making sure HR functions as a business, just as sales or marketing does. If a company has 30,000 employees and spends upwards of $200 million on healthcare costs, anything that HR does to reduce healthcare costs while maintaining quality affects the company's bottom line and morale. Hence, the HR executive operates as a business leader, just as any department head does, and contributes to bottom-line initiatives.

Of course, HR adds value in other ways, too. If the HR executive specifically recruited the leader of a subsidiary and that CEO proceeds to generate millions of dollars in revenue, then HR is playing a major role in boosting the company's revenue. There's more to what an HR executive contributes than cutting healthcare costs or boosting the healthcare plan.

Traps to Avoid

- *Naysaying.* If the business comes to HR with a problem or request in hiring or training, and the answer time after time from HR is that it can't be done, the business loses faith in HR. In my observations, I've seen too many HR departments operate as naysayers rather than doers. Rather than problem solving and getting the job done, HR is afraid to fail and just says no. Saying yes is the way to win over the business, not negating and rejecting every request.

- *Culture Clashes.* If the HR leader wants to be dynamic, active, and strategic, but the CEO and executive team make it clear that they want a yes person, there won't be a smooth fit. The HR leader must know that there's alignment between the vision of the HR executive and the senior management team. The number-one problem I see between HR and businesses is the discrepancy in how each sees the role of HR. Without alignment and a shared vision, the HR executive will be a misfit rather than a cultural fit.

The best way to determine if the HR leader and the CEO and business leaders mesh is for HR to use the same devices that it employs when interviewing candidates: behavioral interviewing. Ask your CEO, "What role do you see your HR leader playing?" If the answer is paper pusher or form collector, the workplace won't be a good fit for an active, progressive strategist. "What has the HR leader done in the past that has created problems?" If the answer is act like a businessperson and not a support function, again the activist HR leader will likely need to find a happier place to work.

Role of HR at a Nonprofit, College, or Government Agency

Most articles and books focus on strategic HR as executed at Fortune 500 public companies. But what are the main differences performing an HR role at a nonprofit agency, educational institution, government agency, or the military? Robb E. Van Cleave, the chief talent and strategy officer at Columbia Gorge Community College, located in The Dalles, OR, and chairman of the Society for Human Resource Management, says the HR leader at a nonprofit performs a similar strategic role as business. "The only difference between education and the public sector is the profit motive," Van Cleave states. Instead of working with a CEO, the HR director collaborates with the college president or mayor to help set the strategic vision for the future and implement the long-term vision of the college or municipality. The goal of the organization is to provide education or a service, not raise profits for the next quarter. And yet, of course, government agencies and colleges have their own budgets to meet and fund-raising goals to achieve. "You're still trying to find talent to execute your strategic plan," he adds.

Hiring at the Nonprofit

Hence, Van Cleave notes that hiring at a college or nonprofit mirrors what an HR department will do at a profit-making business. Personality tests are given; leadership tests are administered. Interviewing is done to ensure that the faculty member and the college's leadership share a similar commitment to education. "We're looking for knowledge, skills, and abilities," he says.

However, Van Cleave also stresses that when hiring, a community college or university is also seeking someone who can connect with students and convey a passion toward learning and teaching. "Hiring choices often come down to choosing someone who possesses emotional intelligence. Before Daniel Goleman's book, we knew it existed but didn't know exactly what to call it," Van Cleave asserts. Universities perform "due diligence" on each candidate, review their scholarship work, investigate their educational background, and contact references. "Often we're looking for a candidate with fire in their belly who can connect with students," and those qualities aren't quantifiable and can't be detected in a resume or scholarly paper. "After the doing the due diligence, it comes down to a visceral gut feeling," he says.

Becoming Strategic at a Nonprofit

Because so many HR directors in government have been faced with declining revenue, they've been forced to do more with less in ways that profit-making companies haven't had to deal with. Recently because of the economic crisis and extensive lay-offs, profit-making companies have caught up. Nonprofit HR leaders learn to hire people who can multitask and ensure that the person fits the job because often there is no back-up or bench strength to cover for first-line employees.

While Fortune 500 HR leaders have to maneuver to gain a seat at the table, at government agencies as well as many nonprofits and colleges, HR leaders must be involved in strategic decision making because resources are so stretched. HR leaders must sit at the table with the college president or the mayor and help execute the vision because HR is at the forefront of stretching the organization's budget and hiring with limited funding, Van Cleave notes.

What Is Expected of HR in a Nonprofit

Since most nonprofits run lean with little support staff, HR must lead, set the agenda, and take an activist's role in setting strategy. There's no time to be wasted. HR must seize the initiative, work with the president or executive director, and collaborate on policy with other organizational leaders. The effective HR executive at a nonprofit cannot be passive, reactive, or cautious. That won't work. Identifying and recruiting the right human capital for the organization will determine its success; hence, HR plays a vital role in propelling the organization forward to achieve its goals. At a large Fortune 500 company, HR may have 142 staff members and there are usually several senior vice presidents leading the organizations. Because decisions may be collaborative, HR leaders often wait to consult with the CEO and other senior management. But at the nonprofit organization, HR must obtain buy-in from senior leaders and act.

Overcoming Pitfalls

In colleges, HR leaders must often deal with territorial issues. The faculty thinks it should make the decision, the president contends that the administration has the power, and students also want to be engaged in making decisions. HR can often serve as a leader since it is one of the few departments that interacts with the entire college, knows and understands how individual departments operate, and can see the college as a whole, not just from one department's viewpoint. For example, at Columbia Gorge Community College, Van Cleave co-chairs a strategic committee with the head of IT at the college. "Our committee crosses all boundaries ... and works with all departments in the college," he says. "But to make a strategic plan work, the committee has to tear down silos, break down walls that separate departments, and work across division lines," Van Cleave notes.

Forming Partnerships with Business Units at Aflac

Audrey Boone Tillman, the executive vice president of corporate services at Aflac (originally named American Family Life Assurance Co.) based in Columbus, GA, oversees human resources management for 4,400 employees, manages 210 total staff, and co-ordinates with businesses in health services, corporate training and leadership, and facilities. "HR touches every business at Aflac," she says. Prior to moving into HR, Tillman was a vice president in the legal department, so she brings her legal expertise into the HR specialty.

Asked what a business unit should expect from HR, Tillman doesn't skip a beat: "They should expect a strong HR/business partnership," she says. The relationship between HR and the business is based on "HR's understanding of the business and the needs of management in the business." For that partnership to thrive, HR must be business savvy; it must understand the overall mission of the business and the specific goals of each business unit. To cement that partnership, Tillman refers to each business unit as a customer and trains her HR staff to specialize in customer service.

Once HR is accepted into the business, the relationship solidifies and deepens. When communication between HR and the business units is open and constant, "HR can be proactive," Tillman says, anticipating the ever-changing business needs of the various business units and working with them to meet Aflac's overall goals. "The sole purpose of HR is to make the business successful," Tillman notes. Because the HR leader adopts that viewpoint and infuses the HR staff with it, business units at Aflac wouldn't think of holding a meeting without HR. In fact, the business managers come to HR to ask who else should participate in their meetings, Tillman suggests. HR's role is to consult, partner, and assist with the business, she stresses.

If People Are Our Most Important Asset, then HR Plays a Significant Role

In an interview with *HR Management* magazine about why he hired Audrey Tillman, Aflac CEO Dan Amos said, "The engine of a company is the people. Hence you need to put your strongest people in the HR department." As a senior associate counsel, Tillman had HR as a client and impressed CEO Amos. When he offered her the job of senior vice president of HR in 2001, Tillman was surprised and not certain that she wanted to move out of the legal department. When she informed her mentor that she was considering turning down the job because she didn't want to relinquish her work-life balance, he replied, "If that's your top priority, then you *should* be the head of HR." Tillman has been dedicated to developing partnerships with business units since she was hired. Indeed, Tillman's emphasis on work-life balance with Aflac's staff helps to retain and motivate employees.

Where HR Went Wrong in the Past

In Tillman's view, the reason HR has triggered so much enmity in the past was that many HR departments operated as policemen, naysayers, or gatekeepers, adopting an attitude of "I'm here to tell you what you can and cannot do." What business wants to partner with a department that is judging it, assuming a negative outlook, and acting in a way to thwart the business from achieving its goals? Is it no wonder the *Fast Company* article "Why We Hate HR" triggered so much acceptance?

HR achieves full partnership when it acts as a problem-solver to help the business unit operate more effectively and achieve its outcomes. For that close relationship to happen, going to HR must be viewed as a positive. HR cannot play a collaborative role with the business if business units think that going to HR is a painful and bureaucratic experience, like visiting the Department of Motor Vehicles or the Social Security Administration office.

HR can offer major assistance with the most important area of any business: its people. Tillman notes that "90 percent of the angst that occurs in management has to do with its people." It's not the building, the cubicles, the cafeteria (though some people will complain about that); it's the people, stupid, to paraphrase a former president. People issues are what vex management and trigger the most conflict. If HR is the people expert and can help the business recruit, motivate, and retain employees, it will be welcome at the table and operate as a full partner.

Knowing the Business Is Crucial

For HR to operate as a problem-solver, not a policeman, it must understand all the nuances of the business unit. It must know the operation and personnel needs of that business as thoroughly as management does. For example, when the Aflac call center was facing issues with "blockage," the term used for customers waiting to speak to a call center representative and getting a busy signal, HR investigated the issue, spoke to call center reps and call center management, and as a result of the feedback, collaborated with the business unit to solve the problem. With the advice and counsel of HR, blockage was decreased to zero waiting time and customer satisfaction rose.

Similarly, when HR was asked to do recruiting for the midnight shift of the Aflac call center, it didn't just fill a recruiting order like a waitress serving ham and eggs for breakfast. "We've got to do substantive customer research to find out what kind people do best at this late shift," Tillman says. Before embarking on a job search, HR completed a profile of the ideal candidate, interviewed successful workers on the late shift, and created a portrait of the ideal candidate. Tillman illustrates all of my earlier points: know HR, do HR, align HR, and assess and quantify issues.

Why HR Must Impact the Bottom Line

"HR has to prove that it can make an impact on the bottom line," Tillman emphasizes. For example, though Aflac was an industry leader on staff retention, HR conducted an investigation into its turnover and sought to quantify its effect on the bottom line. HR determined that every one percent increase in turnover costs the company roughly $1 million in training, recruiting, and advertising costs across the board. HR conducted more extensive exit interviews, led focus groups, and made recommendations to reduce turnover. As a result of HR's and the business unit's working collaboratively, turnover fell more than four percentage points over four years, saving the company millions of dollars. That's a real bottom-line effect.

Even though HR sees itself as a full partner of the business, it sometimes must say no to a business request. Since HR often oversees company policy, maintains the company's brand, and ensures that it operates as an honest, ethical company with integrity, it may on occasion tell the business that what it's thinking of doing is circumventing a rule. Had HR at Enron operated in a consultative way and engaged in constant dialogue with the business, it would have been aware of some of the business practices that lacked integrity and said no to some of its illegal schemes, Tillman suggests.

HR also has to know its limitations. "We can't program computers, process claims, or make sales," Tillman says. But HR can improve how the company's businesses operate and supply them with the best talent. By focusing on recruiting the right people, training and developing them, motivating and retaining them, and delivering on HR promises, it can offer superior customer service to its business units. "Our role is service; our role is to make their job easier," she says.

Everything HR does is focused on improving business outcomes. For example, when HR issues new performance appraisals, it collaborates with the business to focus on how these appraisals will help business maximize its results, improve revenue, operate more effectively, and find new business. What impact will these appraisals have on employees? How will it help Aflac operate in a more effective and efficient way? How will it help HR's customers—the business units?

Training HR Staff

Just as HR plays a critical role in training the Aflac staff, Tillman must instill her customer service approach in the HR staff. Hiring the right people is the starting point. Tillman says that she personally interviews every HR person hired in her department to ensure that they possess the right characteristics to operate in her business

model: offering customer service, listening to clients, and collaborating with customers, not operating as watch guards. Furthermore, she expects that they are business savvy and can operate in
a consultative role, not "I told you so" mode. She models behavior that she expects her HR staff to exhibit, holds quarterly meetings to reinforce points, and keeps HR staff appraised of Aflac's
changing business goals.

Avoiding the Traps

Too many HR executives see themselves solely as gatekeepers
and policy enforcers and prefer to say no, rather than collaborating with businesses to problem-solve and advance the business.
Tillman's advice:

- ☞ *Ease up on operating as the enforcer.* If what the business
  is asking for isn't illegal, immoral, and doesn't break any
  rules, why is HR thwarting its suggestion? Avoid having
  HR operate as a constant roadblock. If HR defines itself
  as saying "no" most of the time, there is no way that the
  business is going to partner with HR.

- ☞ *Instead of putting up roadblocks, help the business achieve
  its outcomes.* What can HR do to make the business operate more effectively? What can it do to help business
  managers attain goals? Improve their hiring, training,
  and development?

- ☞ *View the business and HR as one.* What benefits HR helps
  the business. Helping the business is good for the entire
  company. See issues from the entire company's viewpoint,
  not just the vantage point of what's best for HR.

How an Executive Recruiter Views HR Leaders

Natalie H. Brooks, a managing director of ZRG Inc., an executive search and HR consulting firm based in Newtown, PA, specializes in recruiting HR vice presidents and managers in a variety of businesses including pharmaceuticals, publishing, education, and equipment leasing. Moreover, she's been a talent acquisitions consultant at Creative Human Resources, a partner at several boutique-recruiting firms, and VP of human resources for financial services organizations. Brooks identifies HR talent and determines whether they have the right temperament and skills to fit into an organization's culture. Brooks must understand exactly what kind of HR professional a business wants, and she will be the first to tell you that businesses want and expect different candidates.

What Businesses Want from an HR Leader

Some organizations are seeking a nuts-and-bolts HR executive who follows directions and takes cues from the CEO and business leaders. While some might consider this view of HR as antiquated and retrograde, if the business demands an old-fashioned personnel director to fit into its culture, Brooks will seek out that kind of person. Some CEOs say flat out that they don't want a "player" as an HR executive—that is, an HR manager who is empowered, an independent force, and a dynamic advocate for the department. These CEOs want to control HR and not contend with an outspoken leader, so they hire a more passive or "reactive" HR manager. Management controls this HR manager, explains the problem, and tells the HR vice president how it expects the problem to be solved. The HR leader isn't a strategic thinker but an executor who does what management asks. Obviously the independent thinking, dynamic HR leaders would not be a good fit for this organization.

Many CEOs, however, prefer to hire an HR leader who partners with respective businesses. "They want somebody who *gets* the business," Brooks says, someone who understands the nuances of the business, can work closely with other executives to hire the right staff, and can lead the way in helping the business boost revenue and adapt to a changing business climate. These CEOs think business first and want to bring HR to the table to serve as a human resources leader in the firm. Moreover, they seek an outspoken HR leader who can be an advocate of the business (not HR) and guide the business to operate in a legal and ethical framework.

Through her structured and behavioral questioning, Brooks can identify whether an HR candidate has the experience, know-how, and savvy to serve as an HR business partner. For example, she asks an HR candidate, "In what ways were you involved in helping the business restructure?" If the candidate answers in a limited, tactical way, Brooks may surmise that the applicant isn't ready to serve as partner to the business. If the answers are strategic and reveal that the person initiated a plan and served as point person for the restructuring, and that the plan boosted revenue, it proves the candidate has the backbone and experience to handle the job.

Where HR Executives Go Wrong

Brooks reveals that some experienced candidates possess limited knowledge about the intricacies of the business of their current employer. "I'm shocked by how many HR executives know little about the industry they're in and little about the overall company," she says. She sees many HR executives who can't operate as an HR partner but only focus on the minutia of HR, have a myopic view of what HR does, and can only be placed in positions where the CEO wants a personnel director to handle forms. In most cases, however, Brooks is looking for an HR leader who understands the company's business, can describe its competitive advantage, and knows where it stands in the marketplace and what it has to do to surmount its competitors.

What an Executive Recruiter Expects from an HR Leader

To compete for top-level HR vice president and management jobs at a firm that is pursuing an HR partner, Brooks seeks an experienced professional who possesses "innate business skills, can read financial statements, connect with the business, and become a part of it." In 2009, HR leaders must also demonstrate entrepreneurial expertise and know-how to maximize business revenue. They need to possess the capabilities to oversee a multimillion-dollar HR budget and help the business identify new markets, increase sales, and hire the best people—the full package of skills. The new HR leader works closely with the business on talent management and other HR issues to move the company forward.

Even when HR becomes a part of the business, the HR leader still has the right to disagree with a tack the business is taking. The HR manager retains the right to disagree, state an opposing viewpoint, and explain why the new policy may not be the best for staff morale. Working with the business doesn't mean turning into a "yes" person but maintaining one's independent viewpoint, despite becoming a partner.

Germane to being an HR leader is possessing HR knowledge and expertise. HR leaders must know the HR business, be able to run HR as a business itself, ask the right questions, and admit that the HR leader doesn't know everything.

HR executives who partner with the business also assess what HR does; that is, they are willing to take a critical look at HR activities to improve the business. Too many HR leaders "operate in a defensive mode and are so focused on validating themselves and showing what they're doing is right" that they're afraid to assess their efforts, Brooks notes. The confident HR leader can assess the HR department's actions, admit when a mistake happens, learn from it, reevaluate a policy, and make changes.

Most organizations looking to hire an independent HR leader pursue a person with proven skills in talent management. These HR candidates must demonstrate that they have hired talent that has moved the company forward. HR applicants answer questions such as: What kind of recruiting strategy did they develop in their previous positions? What innovative approaches did they employ? How have they helped the business open new subsidiaries? Have they hired salespeople who raised revenue or assessed how well their sales hiring did?

For example, Brooks once placed an HR vice president at an energy company that was going through a dramatic transformation of its business model. The CEO ultimately selected the candidate because she was outspoken, independent, and performed a similar transformation in her previous company. Though the CEO was supportive of this HR leader as a change agent, the directors beneath the CEO were from the old school. They preferred a more passive HR manager, despite the company's facing massive restructuring and changes that required bolder leadership. They, in fact, preferred the status quo and were as unmovable as a two-ton block of granite.

Some HR leaders would have buckled under the pressure, taken in their sails, given up, or left the company. But this HR leader was not only dynamic and experienced, but also savvy, with a thick skin. She was determined to accomplish her goals, move the energy company forward, and not be deterred by old-school thinking. Strategically, this HR executive devised several solutions to attain her goals, despite confronting resistance from most members of the management team.

In fact, she determined that the command-and-control method displayed by most senior managers needed to change. She encouraged senior executives to act more independently rather than come under the control of the COO. Some of them made the adjustment, and some fell by the wayside. Once a more traditional senior manager departed, she hired new talent that was more open to a more assertive leadership style.

HR managers must also be strategic and politically astute. This HR executive also met with her company's board to alert them of future organizational changes and alterations in strategy and to get them on board as a partner.

Another tactic she employed was meeting with the managers below the director's level to get their buy-in to her new management style. She explained why changing HR policy and transforming the company was critical to its future. She gained their support on changes she expected to make. After the directors initially stomped their feet and resisted, some of them gradually came on board and changed. Some others, however, left the company or were dismissed because they were obstacles to change and viewed as impediments. Strategic, dynamic, independent, and not deterred by resistance, this HR manager was a true leader.

Traps HR Leaders Must Avoid

Where do most HR people go wrong? Here's what Natalie Brooks has learned in her years as an experienced HR executive recruiter.

Trap 1: *Getting Mired in One Fixed Way of Thinking.* Too many HR leaders work at a large company for ten to fifteen years and gradually (and often imperceptibly) become mired in operating in the status quo way. The business world may be changing, the business is going global, the competition has heated up, the market share is declining, and these HR dinosaurs refuse to change. If the HR leader has only one quill in the archery kit and can't adjust to a changing marketplace, this HR leader, if ever dismissed, will never be able to fit into another organization.

Trap 2: *Becoming the Defensive HR Leader.* Some HR leaders see their number-one mission in life as saying no to most proposals. "You can't do that" becomes their mantra. "They use their armor and shield" to fend off any new requests, Brooks observes. And after most business leaders receive one negative response to their suggestion, followed by another "no," they stop coming to HR for anything. HR builds a moat around its office and sends the message to business leaders to keep away. These HR leaders stop innovating, don't adapt to a changing business climate, and become stuck in quicksand. But the HR leaders who operate as trusted partners never operate this way, Brooks adds.

Trap 3: Avoiding Innovation. Settled in their ways and unable to adapt, too many HR people are afraid to take any risks or make mistakes. The dynamic HR leader, working with business partners, investigates new ways to recruit, find, and keep talent and train leaders. The dynamic HR leader never gets stuck in doing things only one way. Thinking outside the box is just as important in HR as it is to an organization's developing new products and markets.

Trap 4: Failing to Speak Up. Some HR leaders are afraid to ever disagree with their business partners. Fearful of losing their job or the respect of other executives, they withhold their true opinion, refuse to offer HR expertise, and acquiesce to business leaders. They lack courage, which moves us to chapter 7, where we'll see how being courageous is the ultimate test of an HR leader.

Hence, if you can avoid all of these traps, you can begin to lead HR and show courage, the subject of our final chapter.

CHAPTER SEVEN

♦ ♦ ♦

BEING COURAGEOUS:
THE ULTIMATE TEST OF HR

Sure, HR has to know its stuff, execute HR, align with the business, and assess its efforts. But all of that is only a starting point. If HR is to be truly effective, it must show backbone, fortitude, a point of view, and most of all, courage. If HR is to be a force in the organization, it can't just blindly follow what the CEO or executive team asks it to do. It must stand up for what it believes in, confront difficult issues, and often act as the conscience of the company.

Why a Courageous HR Matters

Encouraging HR to become courageous has become a passion of mine. I've been on a mission to change the way HR thinks about itself and how organizations view HR. And there's a personal story that underlies this quest.

When I was an associate general counsel at Blockbuster in the early 1990s, I was asked to accept a promotion to become Blockbuster's vice president of HR for the North American business. For almost a week, I struggled internally with whether this "promotion" was really beneficial to me and whether it advanced my career—VP title notwithstanding. Did I, for example, want to give up law, which garnered me so much respect, to move into unchartered territory in HR? It was a difficult decision, but I finally decided to accept the HR appointment because it offered the opportunity to make my mark on a company by influencing hiring, changing policy, and building and developing a strong culture for what was then a small, rapidly growing company.

I vividly recall calling my grandmother, a schoolteacher of forty-six years in Broward County, FL, to tell her about my new position in HR. As opposed to showering me with praise and her normal "That's my boy," her initial reaction was: "Why are you doing that? Why would anyone in their right mind leave a profession (law) and go be a personnel guy?" She couldn't understand why I was relinquishing the status that comes with being an attorney and associate general counsel to move into HR. Human resources, in her view, gets little respect, and I bet her reactions were based on her own experiences with the "personnel department."

Why did I relinquish the status of working as a corporate attorney to move into the much maligned HR department? Having worked in corporate America for several years, I had a vision of what HR could accomplish. I knew HR could be on the cutting-edge of making a company thrive. HR, when done right, could make an organization more successful than it could ever imagine. If organizations truly understood the potential of what great HR could help them accomplish, HR could become the catalyst to transform them into innovative, progressive, forward-thinking juggernauts.

Not long after taking on my new role, though, I quickly began to realize that growing companies are only successful because of their people—the people who dream up the business concepts, design them, market and sell them to consumers. As a vice president of HR at Blockbuster, I realized that the company wasn't really about movie rental; it was about the thousands of people in stores across the country providing an amazing guest experience when people walked through the doors. It reminds me of Herb Kelleher, the founder of Southwest Airlines, saying that his company wasn't in the airline business, but in the customer service and people business.

With this new perspective—my job was to convince the very best people to come join Blockbuster (and remain with Blockbuster) so that we could build a successful business serving our customers— I was off to the races. Now HR was not operating as a business support function; we were ultimately responsible for making sure the business could succeed at all. If the people who operated our retail stores could run them effectively, our business would thrive. If HR could choose the right people, train them, get them to open the stores on time, encourage them to connect with customers, make sure they were honest, reliable, and trustworthy (and didn't steal), and develop them into the next generation of talented managers, Blockbuster's revenue would rise. In short, HR could become the engine that drove the company forward. Now *this was an exciting task*—one well worth giving up my fancy legal role.

So I joined HR with the mission to make it shine by convincing the CEO and senior management team that HR could help drive the business. We were not going to be the lone wolf, but would work collaboratively with the senior management team and employees to pursue business success. HR, with the strong and un-wavering support of the CEO and a strong working relationship with the senior executive team, could and would take on our mar-ket competition. By demonstrating how we could recruit people effectively, develop the best managers, and retain people longer, I knew HR could be a changing force at Blockbuster. I also recog-nized that it would take courage to take a stand, build expecta-tions, and deliver results.

Why the HR Leader Has to Take a Stand

Here's a story that demonstrates the necessity for HR to show courage. I recall an incident at one organization where the HR executive didn't exert enough influence and ended up damaging the company's reputation internally and externally. This company had a good but not great year. The senior management team was only going to hit about 80 percent of their milestones, which meant they'd likely lose about 20 percent of their bonus-earning potential. During a senior management meeting attended by the CEO, CFO, the general counsel, and the chief people officer, the CFO suggested a brilliant idea to save the year (that is, preserve the bonus pool). He suggested that cutting retirees' benefits would save enough costs to help them achieve the necessary operating profit goal to get full bonuses for all. Immediately, the general counsel confirmed that the company could legally do it since they reserved the right to change benefit offerings whenever they wanted to and for whatever reason—after all, these people no longer work for the company, anyway. The HR executive did not take a position on this issue, instead allowing the business people to sort this one out because it was a *business matter*. Instead of taking a position, he simply waited for a decision to be made so that he and his team could work on how best to communicate the change in benefits to the affected former employees. Indeed, when the management team explored the issue and discovered it was legal and could be done, the healthcare benefits of retirees were slashed.

After the cutting of retirees' benefits became known, the staff and the community were up in arms. Staff members wrote e-mails to the CEO, the local newspaper reported the story, and a publicity blitz questioned the company's heart. The turnover rate rose, and the company faced a more difficult time recruiting new staff. What that company learned was that the people who were most affected weren't just retirees, as the senior executive suggested, but the current employees of the company, who felt betrayed. Why stay at a company that was going to make promises and then stab you in the back, many employees thought? If they cut retirees' benefits, they're going to cut mine. Morale sank, and the company floundered. Many employees wondered where HR was, and why the HR senior executive didn't stand up for employees, current and past. The point here is clear: There are times when an HR executive's failure to show courage can have a very negative impact on employees and the employer.

HR Executive as Business Leader

HR executives have to understand that they, too, are business people. In my view, everyone around the senior management table is a business person with some expertise to bring to the business discussion. The CFO is a *business person* with finance expertise; the CMO is a *business person* with marketing expertise; and, yes, the HR executive is a *business person* with people expertise. Of these positions, no one has the lock on who is more important and critical to the business. When HR begins to understand this fact, believes in its own power and expertise, and operates that way within the organization, it will impact the organization. As long as the HR mindset is that it is inferior and not as valuable as other C-suite functions, it will be ineffective and no one will listen to HR. The new business realities demand more courage from HR.

My goal is to encourage HR leaders to take a stand, maintain their independence, represent the company, and advocate for employees. But I'm not suggesting that every HR senior executive turn into the equivalent of "Norma Rae," the rebel-rouser in the film of the same name who vowed to shake up a company. Shouting, screaming, and protesting are not the actions that I'm urging for most HR leaders. An HR leader, in fact, may never have to raise her voice or act in a defiant way, but can use a collegial, consensus-building approach to be effective. What's most critical is that HR senior executives find a way to balance their obligations to the company and to its employees, and all the while help to maximize shareholder value.

Showing the Courage to
Go Against Conventional Wisdom

In fall 2008, the U.S. economy was suffering from a series of failures. Lehman Brothers declared bankruptcy. Bear Stearns was taken over by JPMorgan Chase. American International Group (AIG), Fannie Mae, and Freddie Mae were bailed out by the federal government. The knee-jerk reaction of many conventional HR senior executives would be to recommend to the CEO that the company downsize to curtail overhead and cut costs. Those are actions of HR senior executives who follow the herd. But what would the courageous HR executive do? The courageous HR executive of a financial services company, for example (or a company in another industry, since many businesses are affected by the credit crisis), might have a better idea.

Instead of reducing the company's talent acquisition efforts, the HR executive should propose the company do just the opposite— ramp up recruitment efforts. Why? As a result of the mass layoffs (or threats of them coming) all over the country right now, the market is filled with extremely talented people who are out of work or not secure in their current organizations. A courageous HR professional would propose embarking upon an ambitious plan to rank its current employee base on an A to F scale and use this opportunity to upgrade its talent base by recruiting now-available A and B talent outside of the company to replace its current C, D, and F employees. Enlightened HR leaders would seize the opportunity to acquire really strong talent now so that their organizations will be poised to soar when the economy rebounds.

Why should the HR executive exhibit courage? Most HR executives—not to mention most managers—play it safe. They avoid taking risks, do what everybody else is doing, maintain a low profile, and try not to make waves. There's one major problem with the low-risk, conventional approach: The organization doesn't advance, doesn't outdo its competitors, and isn't structured to win. Business, like sports, is about winning.

The courageous HR executive would attempt to manage risk by eliminating some of the organization's poor performers, then take assertive action by hiring the best and brightest who were suddenly available in the job market. Also, this HR executive thinks like a business person. Instead of just observing the current landscape, this HR top executive recognizes that in six months to a year, the stock market would bounce back, business would pick up, revenue would rise, and the companies that nabbed the best performers in the marketplace would be at a huge competitive advantage because they had the best and brightest minds primed and ready to go.

The Qualities of a Courageous HR Top Executive

So what exactly do I mean by a courageous HR executive? What are some of the qualities and attributes that need to be demonstrated to show courage from an HR leader?

1. *Act as a leader.* Most HR executives follow. They follow trends, other HR people who've always done it a particular way, and other business leaders who tell them what to do. Trends are good as a data point, but not to be followed. Other HR leaders *may* be doing it right and probably aren't, so following them doesn't generally make sense. And if you are simply taking orders from other business leaders (e.g., the CFO, CMO), you are not the HR expert—they are. Let me be clear here: If your HR

leader is following, your organization is not getting the best HR advice and counsel.

2. *Create a culture that works.* Every company creates its own corporate culture. Southwest Airlines differs from American Airlines. Microsoft is distinctive from Yahoo and Google. IBM and Accenture (formerly Andersen Consulting) have different cultures. The courageous HR leader takes ownership in culture—working closely with the CEO—and plays a major role building a climate that can make the difference between winning and falling behind the curve.

   The HR executive at Apple, for example, contributed to creating a culture where people could innovate, take risks, and be rewarded. The HR executive at Research In Motion (RIM) hired designers who invented the BlackBerry and created a technological culture all its own. The HR leaders at Goldman Sachs have always hired not just bean counters but financial innovators. Part of the success of those companies stems from HR executives who had an eye for talent and a strategy to snare people.

3. *Consider future goals.* Most HR executives just try to get through the day unscathed. If the CEO hasn't attacked them and senior managers belittled them, it's been a decent day. But the courageous HR executive isn't just focused on today; this HR leader considers long-term goals, connects with future strategies, and builds revenue for the future, not just the next quarterly earnings report. The courageous HR leader knows HR decisions today could well impact the organization for years to come. As such,

many HR initiatives have long-term payoff and should be openly described to the senior management team. It takes a lot of courage to ask people to spend $10 today and not get a return for five years, but HR leaders do this in business every day.

4. *Possess the courage of your convictions.* Many HR executives second-guess themselves. Unsure of their own beliefs, they wait for signals or orders from the CEO and senior management team. Courageous HR executives have a strategy and game plan in place of how to lead human resources, what kind of people they want to hire, and how to gain their organization's competitive edge through hiring. And, like Nike put it best, courageous HR leaders "Just do it!"

5. *Adapt to a changing business environment.* Some HR executives are stuck in the past. This is the way it was done yesterday, and we'll continue to do it this way. That kind of intransigence won't work in a changing business environment. HR executives who act courageously consider new strategies based on global conditions, new competitors, introducing new product, and rising or declining market share. The best leaders I know have accepted two truisms. First, there's no such thing as staying in the same spot in business; you're either advancing or falling behind. And second, it's sheer lunacy to continue doing the same thing and expect different results. The business world is changing so quickly that HR executives who do not fully embrace change will fail themselves and the organizations they serve.

6. *Hold HR staff accountable.* Despite popular belief, courageous HR executives don't always act as Mr. Nice Guy or Ms. Friendly. The HR function is mission-critical and therefore requires the absolute best HR staff to pull off the work. Gone are the days when the guy who failed in finance or the woman who didn't quite cut it in marketing could find a home in HR. Courageous HR leaders go to the best colleges and universities to recruit their stars, and they recruit seasoned professionals from the list of 100 Best Companies to Work For in America. In short, even the most well-prepared and well-intentioned HR executive can't lead a team of subpar HR professionals to success. Holding people accountable is part of the job.

7. *Operate with minimal fears.* Old-style HR executives were riddled with fears. Anxious about losing their job, uncertain about their role in the organization, and often viewed as outsiders, these HR managers operated from a defensive posture. But courageous HR executives lead with a clear direction, set strategy, work with others, believe in their own skills, and can face disagreement. Fear is not the motivating force, but doing what's best for the organization and creating a strong strategy to deal with change are.

8. *Balance two needs simultaneously.* One of the toughest parts of the HR job is to balance expectations from the senior management team that you will do what is best for the company and the equally strongly held belief of the employees that HR is supposed to watch out for their interests and serve as their advocate. Having personally

been in this position often, I can assure you it's no easy
task to master. But I believe what the effective HR leader
does is put the employees first and still manages to balance the company's interests. If, for example, it becomes
necessary for the business to lay off employees, the HR
executive must manage the process in as thoughtful and
humane a way as possible, always understanding that people (the people who were there for the organization in
good times) must be taken care of as much as reasonably
and fiscally possible.

Becoming the Conscience of the Organization

HR executives are often faced with moral dilemmas. Robb E. Van
Cleave, chairman of the Society for Human Resource Management (SHRM) and chief talent and strategy officer at Columbia
Gorge Community College, The Dalles, OR, can speak from experience, because he was once confronted with a situation that
could easily have cost him his job. At a previous job, when he was
working in HR at a government agency, he became aware that the
chair of a county commission was doing something illegal. Imagine Van Cleave's conflict when he, as a government official, had
to confront another official, look him in the eye, and say, "What
you're doing is wrong. If it's not rectified immediately, I may have
to elevate this and take it to the district attorney."

When Van Cleave confronted the official, the accused re-
torted, "You are absolutely not to inform the other elected officials." Holding his ground, Van Cleave gave him a deadline to
acknowledge the wrongdoing to the other officials or Van Cleave

would bring the issue to the district attorney's attention. Again Van Cleave was ordered not to divulge anything. Eventually, the official went to the district attorney on his own and explained what he did wrong, though downplaying the activity and suggesting it wasn't improper. His admission led to a state investigation. Once Van Cleave's involvement became known, state investigators told him that no harm would come to him. The upshot of the incident was that the official was convicted and forced to resign.

Why did Van Cleave risk his job, knowing that repercussions could easily have been taken against him? "You have to look yourself in the mirror every morning. If you're not going to do it, who is going to be harmed? It's the right thing to do. You can't compromise on doing the right thing," he says.

In Van Cleave's situation, the official's actions were investigated and he was forced to resign. Van Cleave kept his job. Doing the right thing did no harm to him and led to a positive outcome.

Facing Delicate Quandaries

HR is often under the gun. If the CEO wants to reduce costs and personnel fees are the highest operating expense, the HR executive is faced with a dilemma. Considered the advocate of the employee but urged by the CEO to reduce costs, what is a responsible and courageous HR executive to do? Blindly lay off people or devise some alternatives? My suggestion would be for the HR leader to see what costs can be cut, reduced, and spared before laying off any staff.

Can the conference budget be cut? Can videoconferencing replace business trips to reduce travel expenses? Most CEOs tell HR leaders to downsize staff and cut the fat. But I've told CEOs that cutting 10 percent of staff cuts into the muscle. And you don't want to cut into the muscle because if you reduce the number of product engineers and erode an organization's new product development, then revenue in the future will certainly decline. The HR director's role therefore is to balance what's best for the company with what's best for the employees. Often it's walking a tightrope, but sometimes the HR leader has to protect the organization from itself.

When Jerry Yang, the CEO of Yahoo, announced in fall 2008 that 10 percent of its global staff had to be cut to keep the company competitive, he was making an argument that reducing staff would keep the company viable in the face of reduced revenue and heightened competition. The HR executive's role in this case would be to make the case that cutting 10 percent of staff preserves the jobs of 90 percent of staff. In addition, the HR executive would explain that two weeks of severance in a tough economy would not be sufficient to tide over laid-off staff until they find their next job. Hence, if staff cuts had to be made and there was no other viable alternative, the HR leader would ensure that it was done with dignity and respect, not with e-mail messages notifying staff to pack their belongings and leave the building by lunchtime.

Gaining the Confidence of the CEO and Senior Management Team

Showing courage is necessary for the HR executive to perform at maximum level. One way to encourage this behavior is for the HR executive to partner with the CEO and the management team. For many HR executives, gaining the confidence of the CEO and senior management is a critical factor in strengthening their role in the organization. In my view, the most effective way to gain senior management's confidence is to become the HR expert, so everyone on staff comes to rely on the HR leader for guidance and counsel as the people subject-matter expert.

When I give keynote speeches, one of the most popular questions that HR staff members ask is: How do I become well respected? How can I prove my worth to the organization? I've got a clear-cut answer to these questions, and my response is inspired by a visit to my house by a plumber. Yes, a plumber.

Water was gushing out of some pipes in my house, and I was fearful that my belongings or the house's structure were going to be damaged. When the plumber rang my doorbell, he looked a little disheveled and, to be honest, didn't immediately instill confidence in me. However, he moved quickly into the house, observed the water gushing, took out his toolkit, and assessed the situation. Within ten minutes he had stopped the water from surging, repaired the hole, and solved the problem. Guess what? If I had another plumbing problem, I'd call him in a minute. Why? Because he proved he was an expert and solved the problem. That's exactly what a CEO expects from an HR executive.

Becoming an Expert

Just as the plumber assessed the situation, came up with a solution, and fixed the problem, so must HR. HR must be able to analyze problems and solve them. It can't offer a wishy-washy, un-sure, and uninformed response. When business management faces a problem in hiring, needs a viewpoint on whether the CEO is living up to the job, or wants to know how to hire the most inno-vative IT people, the HR executive must be equipped to answer the question, analyze the problem, and solve it. The more compe-tent and resourceful the HR executive is, the more the CEO will offer support and rely on the HR leader.

What Happens to Many HR Executives Who Finally Gain a Seat at the Proverbial Table

Many HR executives spend a considerable amount of time striv-ing to gain the respect of the CEO, build rapport with the senior management team, and gain a "seat at the table." Personally, I am frustrated by the "seat at the table" pursuit because all too often, once we get there, we feel so indebted to be there and to finally have respect and recognition that we become tentative and silent. Rather than using the acceptance to become a rea-soned business executive who serves as a voice for HR and a rep-resentative of the people, the uncertain HR executive clams up and becomes timid. Too often, the HR executive is afraid of mak-ing a mistake or suggesting a recommendation that will backfire and cost him that seat at that table. Frankly, if HR is done right and courageously, you won't have to work that hard for a seat—they'll be begging you to come to the table. But, if you have worked hard to finally arrive at the senior management meeting, when you arrive you must speak up, assert yourself, and not relin-quish your backbone.

When Does Showing Courage Begin?

Most people think that it must take a very long time for the HR executive to build up political strength, gain allies, and show the expertise needed to demonstrate courage. But I disagree. In my view, if the HR leader is going to show courage, it all starts when the HR leader is being recruited by an organization. Let me explain.

I received a call from an executive recruiter describing the "perfect" HR job. The company was outperforming its competitors, they had a dynamic CEO who "got HR" and wanted to support a strategic HR executive, and most important, money was no object. This company would pay whatever it took to get the right HR executive. Although I wasn't looking for a job at the time, I thought I should explore it, so I asked the recruiter to send me the position description and an organizational chart. Upon receiving the requested documents by e-mail, I realized the job description and organizational chart showed the chief HR officer position reporting three levels down in the organization—not direct to the CEO. At that point, I promptly hit the reply button and typed: "No, thank you. If HR were as important and critical as this organization says it is, the position description and the organizational chart would reflect that."

My point here is that the time to evaluate whether HR can have a truly change-oriented role in the organization is at the outset of the relationship. Think about it in the context of dating. Chances are that if someone doesn't show you the things that you value on the first date, marriage shouldn't really be an option. The same holds true for HR leaders looking to transition to new roles. To find out what the organization really thinks about HR, look to its own words—either on the first interview, in the position description, and/or on the organizational chart. I actually rhetorically asked the above-mentioned executive recruiter, "Where do the CFO and the general counsel report within this business?" I must admit it took a lot of courage not to pursue this particular HR job, but I'm better for it, and I submit to anyone reading this who wants to have a successful HR career, look, prod, and ask tons of questions about the organization's commitment to its people and to the HR function.

Courageous HR leaders decline jobs all the time, knowing that money alone will not bring happiness; in fact, the odds are strong that despite the allure of the inflated paycheck, a powerless HR position would lead to real unhappiness and dissatisfaction.

Two Factors That Determine an HR Executive's Courage

To become a powerful force in the organization, HR has to gain the trust of the CEO and senior management team. If the HR executive has the full support of the CEO, it makes it easier to initiate new HR practices, test out new procedures, make a mistake, and learn from it. When John Conaty was HR executive at GE, he had the full backing of Jack Welch, including the financial backing, to create a resourceful leadership center.

Obviously having the support of the CEO makes it easier for the HR executive to exhibit courage. But ultimately HR courage must also come from within. At the end of the day, no one can give you the necessary courage to pull off a difficult job but yourself.

Don't Act Powerless and Defensive

When I was named HR executive at IAC/InterActive Corp., one of CEO Barry Diller's first actions was to invite me to the senior management meeting. Diller didn't need to issue a press release saying that HR was now a force in the organization. His action sent a strong signal to everyone at IAC, from senior management to the janitor, that HR had gained a seat, literally and figuratively, at the table and was going to influence policy and get involved in strategy.

Not only must the HR director act in an assertive way and handle the politics of the organization astutely, but the organization must be open to a changing HR department, too. Whether the organization is a Fortune 500 company, a nonprofit, or a small business, it must welcome and embrace the idea that HR can exert influence on the company's policies because of its role in talent acquisition and retention. If HR is not perceived as a power player, it sends a strong signal to the company that taking care of its people is not a major priority.

Much depends on the actions of the HR executive. If the HR top executive is timid, passive, and fawning toward the CEO and senior management team, then HR will be perceived as weak and ineffectual. But if the HR manager/leader strides when he walks in the room, exudes confidence, understands the organizational power dynamics, adroitly adjusts to a changing business environment, and has the ear of the CEO and management, then the rest of the staff knows that HR is a force to be reckoned with and can represent the staff's best interests.

Too many HR leaders hide from making decisions and taking a stand. Some HR people only want to express their opinion on HR-related issues such as healthcare benefits or employee surveys and avoid taking a stand on anything outside their narrow area of responsibility. Everything that happens in the company affects HR and the staff, so it is imperative that HR take a stand and speak up on any and all issues affecting the organization.

Be Prepared to Contend with Reluctant Senior Managers

Even though some CEOs make it clear that they support their HR departments and are wholly behind them, some senior managers refuse to work with HR. In chapter 1, I told a story about Phil, the editor at a publishing house in New York. This crafty, seasoned, quick-talking guy would say, "Why would I go to HR, all the way on the sixth floor? Does HR know more about editors than I do? I have a Rolodex with some of the leading editors in New York. Why would I need HR's assistance? I call on HR when I need to have a new recruit fill out paperwork. That's all I need from HR."

How would I, the experienced HR executive, convince this seasoned editor that HR can in fact help him recruit talent, despite his lengthy Rolodex? Well, the answer is I wouldn't tell him; I'd show him. First, I'd plan some one-on-one time with Phil to share my prior work experiences and to learn more about his. Then, I'd ask him to let me help him improve the quality and productivity of his hires. I'd have done my homework about Phil's current department and shared with him my turnover research findings about his group of employees versus industry norms. Let's say Phil's department had a 40 percent departure rate in editorial compared to an industry norm of 28 percent annually. I'd inform him that our research shows that each job search for a new editor costs the company $72,000, and since he had to hire eight more editors than the industry norm last year, he was spending an additional $500,000 in recruitment costs. So while his Rolodex may be impressive and his contacts vast, the numbers say Phil's department is falling behind the industry and costing the company a considerable sum.

Moreover, I'd note that 72 percent of the editors who left were between the ages of twenty-five and thirty-five. So Stan and his team may be facing a Generation X and Y problem. I'd suggest special training in this area on how baby boomer managers can improve relationships with Generation Xers. In addition, I'd organize team-building exercises to boost morale and motivate employees, in order to increase and lengthen retention. In short, I'd do everything in my power to win Phil over by showing him that I am expert in people issues and can help him operate better and less expensively; I would act as Phil's people consultant.

Now, ultimately, if all of this didn't convince him, and in rare cases you will encounter managers who absolutely refuse to accept change—especially from an HR person—then I'd use my relationship with the CEO to ensure that everyone gets on board with HR as the leading recruiter. Then it becomes clear that anyone who acts independently of what the CEO asks is not doing what's in the best interests of the company.

Dealing with the Ninety-Day Syndrome

After ninety days on the job and often well before that, the HR executive is going to be tested. Within that first ninety days, a

C-level executive is going to question why HR is surveying employees, encouraging more detailed performance appraisals, introducing coaching to the vice president level and above, or launching a long-term investigation into improving recruitment. Someone will say, "You're just the HR executive. What do you know?" Believe me, you will be questioned. You will be challenged, belittled, and most of all, tested to see what your inner fortitude consists of. In fact, if no one happens to challenge you, I recommend introducing an HR initiative to test the waters. It's always better to know where you stand. Initiate a cutting-edge approach and see how the CEO and management team react. Once you've faced your first crucible and test of courage, you'll have a better idea of where you are positioned in the organization. This doesn't mean you should turn every issue into a battle, of course. Choose your battles carefully.

Why the HR Leader's Courage Affects the Bottom Line

While some executives refer to what HR does as "soft" skills versus the "hard" skills of finance, marketing, and IT, what HR accomplishes affects the bottom line as much, if not more, than the other businesses. Without the best people, the organization will decline and lose its competitive edge. If the HR executive isn't independent, courageous, and effective, the organization will not be able to compete for the best talent. Without the best talent, revenue will decline and the company will lose market share to competitors and ultimately fail. Nothing "soft" about that.

Moreover, HR, as well as legal, can serve as the organization's ethical compass. When Enron senior executives were inflating trades and Arthur Andersen executives were fudging audit reports to sell more consulting services, where was HR? Did HR speak up and explain how these unethical, if not illegal actions might adversely affect the company in the long term? Both of these companies, which had multibillion-dollar revenues, are now defunct, brought down and destroyed by the unethical conduct of their senior executives. These organizations needed a strong HR leader to object to avaricious behavior gone wild. Had HR spoken up and convinced business leaders to change course, those companies might still be operating.

What Can HR Do When the Business Refuses to Stop Its Unethical Behavior?

When I deliver my keynote speech "Be Courageous—The Ultimate Test of HR" before an audience of HR executives and practitioners, I'm frequently asked the what-if question about HR ethics. What if the HR leader questions the unethical behavior of the CEO or management team and the team ignores HR's advice, refuses to budge, and continues its unethical practices, despite the HR executive's emphatic objections?

In my view, the issue is clear: It's time to leave the organization and find an organization that fits with your ethical guidelines. If you are the HR leader of an organization that has turned unethical or corrupt and the CEO and senior leaders won't change their ways, your reputation will be tarnished and besmirched. I jokingly encourage all HR people to keep a "Go to Hell Fund"—just six months or so of your annual compensation tucked away in the event you are faced with working in an environment where people are acting unethically, illegally, or simply unwisely because they don't understand the value of their people. If you can save six months' to a year's salary, you are better off hitting the pavement and looking for a job, even in a tough economy, than staying in an organization where a lack of ethics has become the prevailing business mode.

Why the HR Executive Is as Important as the CFO

Jack Welch, management guru and former CEO of General Electric, understood the importance of HR. As he wrote in *Winning*, "HR has just got to be as important as any other function in a company. In fact, why wouldn't HR be as important as finance? After all, if you managed a baseball team, would you listen more closely to the team accountant or the director of player personnel? Both the accountant and director of player personnel belong, alongside the CEO, at the table where decisions are made." Welch knew that HR could play a strategic role in forging a company's competitive edge.

Welch also noted that there are four major impediments to HR being viewed as a leader in the organization. He said that:

1. Many business leaders think that what HR accomplishes isn't measurable in the way that the sales manager can identify a 10 percent increase in sales.

2. Most CEOs and leaders consider themselves "people" experts and think they know as much about recruiting and identifying talent as the HR leader.

3. HR is viewed narrowly as the "benefits" function.

4. More than any other department, HR gets entwined in "palace intrigue" and has more rumors floating about it than other departments.

Overcoming Jack Welch's Four HR Traps—and Other Traps to Avoid

Let me rebut the traps that Jack Welch mentions and then describe a few others that HR executives must contend with.

Trap 1: HR's Effect Isn't Measurable

I call this the biggest, but in many ways the easiest, hurdle for HR people to deal with—one I've constantly had to address over the years. Several years ago, when metrics was the craze and buzzword in business circles, the CEO of the company I worked for told me that she needed me to do a better job measuring HR's impact on the business. I took her comments to mean she didn't believe we (the HR team) were adding quantifiable value to the company, which, to be honest, made my blood boil. After all of the blood, sweat, and tears the HR professionals of this company had put into making this a successful enterprise, the CEO still didn't get it. So, over the weekend following that conversation, I planned a follow-up conversation with her on Monday. It went like this.

I began the conversation by asking her to think back about eighteen months, prior to the period one of our businesses—let's call it Division A—was not performing well. In fact, Division A was our largest division and was performing so poorly that it dragged down the results of the entire company. During this period, our CEO spent countless hours in meetings with the senior management team to determine if we needed to put more capital dollars into our infrastructure, more dollars into marketing, or if we needed to sell Division A altogether.

One day, during one of our meetings, I told her I had the answer, to which she laughed and asked, "What does the HR guy know about this business problem?" I refrained from saying what I wanted to say ("Well, he can't do any worse than your team!") and instead explained to her that most business problems were not marketing, product, or technology problems; they were people problems. I further explained that no matter how much money she spent marketing Division A to the public, she should not expect change until we replaced the business operator with a better leader. She agreed and allowed me to commence a search for a new president for Division A. And within nine months of hiring Division A's new president, we saw an amazing turnaround, which ultimately benefited the entire company. Division A experienced a $20 million swing toward profitability.

Despite HR's active role in turning the division around, HR received no recognition. As I told her, no one gave credit to the HR professionals who worked tirelessly to recruit Division A's president. No one on the senior management team seemed to understand that the talent acquisition professionals had to find the president, or that the compensation and benefits professionals had to put together a compelling rewards package to attract and induce the president to leave his then-employer, and that the employee relations/generalist professionals had to make sure the new president's family had a smooth relocation experience to the new city, which included marketing their former home so that it sold at a good price, which allowed the company to avoid having to take the home into inventory at a considerable cost.

So, even before Division A's president started, HR's impact was, at least, $170,000 because we (a) didn't use an executive recruiter to find Division A's president ($150,000 savings by HR), and (b) sold his house as opposed to bringing it into inventory ($20,000 carrying costs avoided by company). And then, in just nine months, Division A was a remarkable turnaround story ($20 million). Tell me HR's efforts can't be measured and aren't significant.

I soundly reject any notion that HR, when done right, doesn't produce measurable results. The challenge HR people have is being able to tell the story (talk business jargon and numbers) and "toot their own horns" (take credit for their successes). At the same time, organizational leaders, particularly the top leaders, have to be willing to recognize the fact that the efforts of HR—whether recruiting a game-changing CEO, convincing hard-to-find engineering talent not to leave for an offer from a competitor, or saving the company millions of dollars by renegotiating the healthcare plan contract—significantly impact the organization in measurable ways.

Trap 2: Everyone's a People Expert

If I've heard it once, I've heard it a million times: "I don't need any help from HR. I know people because I've been managing for years." Well, that is about as absurd a notion as naming an employee your CFO because he says he has successfully managed a departmental budget for years. It's silly. Surely, all of us have some experience with hiring and managing people, but that experience does not give us sufficient expertise to be able to perform the very complex roles played by HR professionals in today's environment. Believe it or not, there is actually an HR body of knowledge that, at a minimum, a competent HR person should master. It includes competency in areas such as strategic management, workforce planning and employment, human resource development, compensation and benefits, employee and labor relations, and occupational health, safety, and security. And while it is true that most business leaders understand *conceptually* the dynamics of compensation and recruitment, for example, they don't possess the skills and know-how to develop a strong rewards program that works to keep the brightest and best employees engaged.

It absolutely amazes me how no one would ever hire a chief marketing officer or a chief financial officer who did not possess formal credentials and experience in their fields, but often someone will place an inexperienced "business person" over HR without blinking. Well, everyone doesn't know HR, and organizations that don't understand this fact are not doing right by their organizations. And for those of you reading this right now who are prepared to argue with me by pointing out that they know one non-HR professional who is doing a great job, I'll show you a thousand who aren't and who are really bringing harm to their organizations.

Trap 3: Falling into the Benefits Niche

Yes, HR leaders must ensure "the trains run on time" by taking care of benefits and performance appraisals and ensuring that the basics that employees and employers alike expect are being provided. But that's only a fraction of what an enterprising HR department and leader must accomplish. Successful HR leaders must also be involved in creating strategy, meeting the future needs of the organization, and planning global approaches—all the while providing administrative services like payroll and benefits. I often remind audiences when I speak that, for all the fancy talk about strategic HR, our employees expect to be paid on their regularly scheduled payday and for their health insurance to work when they visit the doctor. Our employees couldn't care less about HR strategy and bench strength analyses when they find themselves sitting in an emergency room at 3 a.m. with a screaming kid, only to learn HR didn't process their benefits paperwork. The real challenge for the HR profession is to perform the nuts-and-bolts HR work, but not be exclusively defined by that. HR people must also be recognized for the strategy work they do that impacts the organization—the work that leads to hiring and retaining the best talent in the marketplace.

Trap 4: Overcoming the Gossipmongers

Let me be clear at the outset. I believe this idea that HR people are big gossipers is overstated. I do, however, believe one HR professional who does not respect people's privacy and who does not maintain confidences is one too many. And when members of the profession learn that another HR professional has violated the professional ethics rules, they should do something about it— much like members of the medical and legal professions do. Because HR has access to the most confidential of information— about salaries and criminal background history, medical conditions and marital disputes—HR professionals must be super careful about divulging, even accidentally, the information they are entrusted with.

In every HR organization I've run, I make it clear from day one that anyone who divulges confidential information in HR will be fired. In fact, when I learned that a member of our HR team, who was an otherwise outstanding and highly effective employee, had disclosed that someone on staff suffered from HIV/AIDS, I immediately terminated his employment. In many ways, it took courage to let the person go because he was liked and respected by most employees; but we established a code of honor, it was breached, and the person had to be held accountable. Because some HR departments don't operate a zero-tolerance policy when it comes to gossip, people like Jack Welch identify this area as a trap for HR—something I find utterly maddening and unacceptable for the profession.

Trap 5: Dealing with the Misperception That HR People Are Only Good at Throwing Parties

Despite all the changes that have transpired in the world of HR, some business leaders persist on seeing HR as the group that is best utilized organizing the holiday party and the company picnic and doing some morale-boosting events. That's it. In their view, HR should leave formulating business strategies to the business leaders. Overcoming that perception requires HR to become a leading expert by initiating strategies that add value and seizing opportunities to add value.

Trap 6: When the CEO Gives Lip Service

Most CEOs sooner or later (usually at the quarterly business meeting) discuss how "people are our most important asset." But often those words are nothing more than lip service when management is faced with a downturn in business. Some of the first things on the chopping block when times get hard are training and development, employee relations, and employee communications. This reality undermines HR because the employees conclude HR doesn't have sufficient clout—or courage—to keep the rest of the management honest. It's the role of the HR executive to step up and ensure that the company lives up to the CEO's words and that employees are not forsaken during tough times.

Trap 7: When HR Doesn't Have Its Act Together

The other major breakdown that undermines HR happens when the HR leader isn't knowledgeable. Unless the HR executive can be depended on as an expert problem-solver, the partnership between HR and the business won't work. HR must be business savvy, know the underpinnings of the business, and be aligned with it. Hence, everything depends on HR as an expert and consultant to help move the business forward.

It's all about courage.

I've known some really sharp people who know HR, execute the fundamentals really well, align themselves with the organization's goals, and assess HR initiatives to determine effectiveness and value. These are very good HR leaders. There are, however, a few great HR leaders who add an element of courage to these attributes. I heard someone say the other day in a church service that "one cannot give a testimony until they have been tested." The HR leaders who have the scars to show they have been in the battle are the ones that are really advancing the profession and taking care of the people who work in the organizations we service.

Truly courageous HR leaders move past just being business partners and become accepted as part of the business. When HR is a part of the business, it is respected as an integral contributor to the bottom line by supplying a steady stream of first-rate talent to the organization. It knows the short-term and long-term goals of the business. It plans ahead to furnish staff and fill expected vacancies, replace managers who leave, and anticipate future staffing and leadership needs. Poised on the front lines, HR provides innovative talent, builds the organization's talent strengths, inspires new products and markets, and adapts to changing business conditions.

When HR works, not only does the organization gain, so does the HR leader. Feeling confident, supported by the CEO, collaborating with the management team, forging positive relationships with staff, the HR executive is able to drive the hiring strategy, groom future leaders, and concentrate on training staff with updated skills—and in the process, the HR executive gains self-satisfaction and fulfillment by helping shape the organization. Living up to one's own potential drives the HR executive to constantly grow, learning new things and adapting to a changing business environment.

When HR is showing courage, the company thrives, the shareholders prosper, and employees are energized—everyone gains.

INDEX

strategic planning (*continued*)
  workforce planning and, 1, 2, 5, 55,
    59, 69, 80–81, 128–130, 168–169,
    207–208
Strategy-Focused Organization, The
    (Kaplan and Norton), 102
Streep, Meryl, 121
subprime mortgage market, 35–36
succession planning, 14, 54, 151
Sunglass Hut, 142

talent acquisition strategy, 33–61
  assembling steps in, 45–46
  boosting impact of talent acquisition
    specialists, 52–53
  building relationships in, 36
  business cycle in, 37, 39–40
  competition for talent and, 15–16,
    35–37, 60, 70–71, 115–116
  competitive edge and, 60
  competitors' stars and, 36–37,
    70–71, 125–126
  corporate culture in, 37–38, 40,
    47–48
  developing, 19–20, 53–54, 107–108
  difficult-to-fill positions in, 48–49,
    55–56, 124, 125–126
  at EMC Corporation, 39–40, 45–49,
    53–54
  emotional intelligence of
    candidates, 23–24, 111–112,
    118–119, 130
  employment brand in, 38, 43–44
  five-step program, 37–46
  Google and, 37–38, 43–44, 57–58
  HR function in, 33–34, 45–61
  at IAC/InterActive Corp., 124,
    125–129
  importance of, 3, 14, 31–32, 35–37
  Internet job sites in, 107–108, 111,
    119–120, 126, 129
  key sources of talent, 36
  labor market trends in, 37, 39–40
  at Nationwide Financial Services,
    39, 44–45, 49–52, 53

new hiring paradigm in, 57–58
objectifying job search in, *see*
    objectifying job searches
proactive approach and, 2, 5, 10–13,
    16–17, 21–23, 28, 31–32, 35–37,
    47–48, 64, 70–71, 128–130
problems with, 35–37
rewards program in, 38–39, 44–45
sales mentality in, 38–39, 44–45, 53
in smaller companies, 35
social networking sites in, 56–57,
    63–64, 70–71, 77, 120
strategic plan in, 38, 40–43, 58,
    101–112
talent coordinator role in, 58–59
talent management in, 46–49
talent scouts in, 12, 34, 78
workforce planning in, 1, 2, 5, 55,
    59, 69, 80–81, 128–130, 168–169,
    207–208
at Yahoo, 38, 39, 40–44, 53–56, 70,
    124, 125–126
see also recruiting employees
TalentKeepers, 82
talent management, in talent
    acquisition strategy, 46–49
talent scouts, in talent acquisition
    strategy, 12, 34, 78
Tanaka, Wendy, 70–71
Target, 134, 144–145
Taylor, Johnny C., Jr., 4
teams
  consensus building and, 117–118
  corporate culture based on, 112
  in hiring strategy, 54–55, 102,
    117–119, 124–128
  pros and cons of, 117–118
  sports, 12, 34, 65–66, 72,
    73, 87
temporary employees, 22, 48
TheLadders.com, 107
theme park businesses, 173–175
360-degree performance standard,
    6, 100, 104–107
behavioral interviews and, 111

www.ingramcontent.com/pod-product-compliance
Lightning Source LLC
Chambersburg PA
CBHW011932190326
41519CB00029B/7499